Alzheimer Diary
A Wife's Journal

Michelle Montgomery

Copyright © 2010 Michelle Montgomery
All rights reserved.

ISBN: 145280706X
ISBN-13: 9781452807065

To My Children, My Starbursts
Katheryn   Patrick   Jennifer

To the memory of my beloved husband
David Kent

To Ray Uloth, who rides with me through
the pain of transition

Prologue

I want our perfect life back, to return to the time we lived it *together*—a time when I would not be fighting my own demons as well as struggling with my husband's descent into mental chaos.

I want another New Year's Eve like our second one together, the jazz club in the Valley where Super Sax was playing. When they put down the first notes, my head exploded.

We danced and danced. I still remember my dress and shoes — apricot trimmed in brown, clingy and short, with tan shoes, mid-heel. Dave was so beautiful and very cool in his safari shirt. He knew who the players were, and, at forty-five, who he was. I was thirty-two.

I cannot catch a whiff of Mennen's *Musk* without remembering that night.

Twenty-five years later he lingered in the doorway of my office, on his face an expression I had never seen before. A little hurt, sad, bewildered.

With a questioning tilt to his head he said, "The doctor tells me I have Alzheimer's. You are supposed to call his office and talk to his nurse. Then come with me on my visits from now on."

Our world shifted. My world shifted.

If only I could re-wind the film.

Four years later I began this diary.

Chapter 1

NOVEMBER 6, 2005

Frustrations.

Find your own goddamn hat. Fifteen times a day I help you look for your hat. I want some time to look for my own hat.

You have no clue where you left your hat. You need it because your head is cold. Your head is always cold.

I hate that you mix up the dirties and the cleans in the dishwasher. And the dirties and the cleans in the wash.

A couple of days ago I insisted, because you complained again of the cold, that you put on your turtleneck instead of the short sleeve summer shirt. You never know the season now, or the weather.

After a while, I came to your room to check on you. You were struggling to put your legs into the arms of the turtleneck after having taken off your sweat pants but still leaving on the short sleeve shirt.

Tonight I commented on how much your kitty loves you, Kitty Rings the one sitting in your lap and who sleeps in your bed—you could not find her until I touched her soft fur to your hand.

This is a damnable and fascinating thing, this Alzheimer's. Where are you disappearing to? I do not like to see your awareness fading because of a bunch of gooey stuff clogging up your neurons—plaques and tangles the doctors call it, but do not know which is the real culprit.

Where is my David now?

For a week or so you complained of this hurt on your chest. Finally, last night, you retrieved the memory that you had fallen in the post office, tripped on a package and fell flat. Usually our people in this small Sam's Valley take such good care of you.

Yesterday when we went to Rainey's, our corner store, the clerks, the owners, came over to say hello to you, *Can I help? Are you finding what you need?* Then they see me. "Oh, you have brought a helper."

I was not needed. Others in their kindness are taking care of you too. Such a relief to know, it frees me from worry when you are gone.

What I need is to learn how to deal with my own emotions.

Is more patience required? No, more compassion.

December 1, 2005

Trapped again, and cranky. Damn back pain, which comes at these times of extreme stress. Why does my body insist on making a hard time worse? Where is my survival instinct?

Last night the snow was so beautiful, reminded me of the days when we reveled in it. When it was more than an obstruction.

Dave drove up our long driveway before lunch to get the paper, as he usually does. He was gone for so long I got a little panicky. Had he decided to go off to Rainey's to get ice cream? Did he slide off the driveway into a ditch?

I was also annoyed—when will he get back so I can be in my life?

Will I have to tramp up the road in the boots that pull on my sore back? Will I have to drive the truck up? I am not a truck person.

Maybe my friend Beth is right...a support group. Maybe our son Patrick is right...an occasional caregiver.

·

Dave is not the only one being enveloped in a cocoon, one of forgetting; I am drawing one around me also, a cocoon of isolation. I do not want intruders, strangers, nor is there anywhere I want to go. I sometimes worry I may leave off loving him, that he may become an obligation rather than my beloved husband.

I know if we ever did spend a week in New York again, staying at the Plaza, drinking dry martinis in the Oak Bar, eating spring lamb and fresh asparagus in the Oak Room—I would be the only one really there, the only one of us who would be weaving in the memories of when we visited that magic place before.

Damn!

December 3, 2005

The constant *war of the door*. The collies Mazie and Meggi sleep near my side of the bed, Cindy the spaniel as close to Dave as she can get. He always leaves during the night to sleep in the guest room; apparently I snore, though he claims to be unsure of why he goes.

When he gets up to go to the bathroom, around five or so, he comes over and closes my door no matter how many times I have asked him not to. Within no time, Cindy scratches to get out. I was asleep, now awake and pissed. I sleep only in few hour segments anyway, but want it to be my rhythm, not an imposed one. Last week I piled boxes against the door, wedging it open. An eyesore, but it worked just fine.

He just cannot remember Cindy will want to come out to be with him. And what is worse, from my standpoint of relishing being upset with him to release my anger, is that he closes the door so I can sleep and not hear him awake and roaming. He is being considerate and I am a shrew.

This morning was surreal.

Last night, precious grand-baby Simone came to sleep over with me. She is now a 'big girl' of four and loves her Grammy time. But at two a.m. she awoke stressed, wanting her mommy, wanting to go home. Kathy soon came for her. I went back to bed and fell asleep for an hour, awake another hour, asleep, another awake, etc.

Then, as daylight began, I sensed the quiet hand moving the door shut. I bolted, told him, "No, leave it open." Back and forth went the door; his knowing the difference between open and closed momentarily blotted out by my irritation.

What I wanted to do was scream, "Open is open! Closed is closed!"

Sigh.

December 4, 2005

Today was a good day. Last night, after writing, I was wrestling with the guilt of focusing more on my own emotions than on him. It is not what I intended when I started writing but being *my* diary, of course it is in large part about that: my pain, my irritation, my inconveniences.

Though because he is the one losing himself, I might ask, almost did, "What right have I to be pissed at him for something he cannot help?" And I would answer, if I had asked, "It's not about right but about being human." I am half of the equation of our new life.

This morning, he closed the door again. Lucky for us both, Cindy snored on, did not scratch to get out. Plus, I had a good night's sleep and dove into housework, which I usually hate, but today it helped me regain control. And the sun was shining.

And at lunch he wanted to give me his part of the paper, over and over. All who know him tell how generous and considerate he is, always offering the chair, the jacket, the bowl of peanuts. That I do not want the door closed, or the heat too high is something he would surely note if he were able.

December 5, 2005

A little bit scary this morning. He was not his usual wake-up-jolly, joking self.

Looking inward, not confused exactly, but pained, though not with physical pain. He is never sick. Once or twice in our thirty years.

When I asked him how he was, he suggested not so good. "Did you sleep okay?" Yes. It's something else he can't identify; I need to be a detective. When he is in a vulnerable spot it is easy for me to be compassionate.

This is like a little lamb looking for its mommy, one of those kittens in the cage at the Humane Society saying, "Take me, take me." Just like Jack, Mickey, and Briquette, how could we take just one?

I have discovered iTunes for 99 cents I can download songs to the music library. I cannot imagine life without music. I cannot imagine writing without a music score behind my telling, my emotions.

Yesterday and today it is *Take My Breath Away*, over and over and over. Remembering how he did indeed take my breath away. *Free Bird* comes right after. I can alter the order, but did not plan it, so fitting, so painful.

Not the same really, the song is about someone leaving intentionally.

If I leave here tomorrow, would you still remember me...

And then Eric Clapton's, *would you know my name... If I saw you in Heaven...*

I seem to be a B-movie queen, able to queue up the sense of my emotions when there is a sound track.

I am ready Mr. DeMille.

So, to the point of that, what I see is there is such a history. This person is attached to me. Attached: as in stuck to.

We used to have fights. I dumped a plate of chili on his head. He decided to sleep in the car, always his resolution to a fight. I thought it was to punish me. Why would he think I would be punished by that? Now in writing this, I see he may have been protecting himself. Am I so fierce? Maybe.

If I were to go daft, I would say this could be payback. Not going to the backseat of the car but the backseat of his mind.

Of course, I'm not yet that daft.

DECEMBER 7, 2005

May Sarton says, "One of the problems of a journal written on the pulse is also that it must be concerned with the immediate, looking back only when the past suddenly becomes relevant in the light of the present moment."

My immediate, present moments are filled with the past. The day I met Dave is so clear in my memory.

1965 - A perfect Old Pasadena summer day. The neighborhood just off of Orange Grove. Big old trees, magnolias with their big blossoms and perfume, big old houses. Shady, not too hot.

I was door-to-door collecting for a fund for MS or MD, don't remember which, just answered the call from some women who had gotten lots of refusals. Door-to-door over several blocks, Patrick in the stroller, eight months old. Dave's was one of the last houses I came to, though across the street from ours. Guess I wanted to land soft, near home.

I was wearing blue, he was wearing blue. Mine was what now seems a silly dress: white and pale royal blue stripes about one and a half inches wide, a sort of sailor collar with a tie in front. He in navy short sleeve shirt, navy shorts. He has beautiful legs; he jumped short hurdles in high school.

Most people gave ten cents, or maybe twenty-five.

He was one of those people, had one of those faces: pure good shone in his smile and openness—it was right there in my face, I saw it even before he handed me the five-dollar bill.

That was the beginning.

December 8, 2005

Balancing our needs. He gives because he is a giver. He reaches and stretches, saying 'yes' even to that which is beyond him.

I give because there are those who need. Sometimes I wonder if many of my feelings are borrowed, absorbed from *the other*, including animals. Apparently it does happen. Those women now live in the loony bin called 'Women Without Borders.'

Tonight we watched an amazing movie, *After Life*. It is about many things, but principally the search for your happiest moment to live in forever, take with you to your after-death place. Dave was either entranced by the beautiful cinematography or indulging me.

I was at times drawn away—to serve dinner, to check if this was okay with him, to let the dog through the door. This was a movie I did not want to leave. Trying to figure out my happiest moment—there are too many, cannot choose. The idea is completely absorbing.

(Intermission, he is standing in the hall wondering where he is to sleep. Okay, quickly resolved. Brush your teeth first, then the pill. His indecision is not as bizarre as it seems since he starts out in our room, but spends most of the night in the guest room.)

Okay, now even more disturbing, I also gave him an anti-diarrhea pill. To his question, I joked, "You didn't know I was a nurse, did you?"

He said, "Did you go to nursing school?"

Oh Lordy, what will become of us?

Actually, in spite of all the changes, I love my life. Each day has its own special magic—I know it is there and take the time more and more these days to open to it.

The ordinary events of today will be what I long for next year; no longer will they be in the realm of possibility.

When I came to bed last night, he was under the covers completely dressed including jacket and boot slippers. He was sort of okay about my taking them off of him, but really does not like to be fussed with.

You know what they say about what you wish for. I used to think I wanted control—I certainly didn't ever want this much.

I was up early, needing to get Mazie to the vet by 8:30, had showered and dressed. He saw me in my 'town' clothes, said, "You look like you are going somewhere."

Yea! Will he recognize that in a year? He still had to ask a couple or more times where I was going. Didn't know where I had been when I came back.

I like it that he knocks at my office door if it is closed. But wonder what he imagines I would be doing that needed privacy.

Adored wild child Simone was here today. Dave seems younger than she sometimes. It is a job keeping the two of them from each other—she is scared of him, but provokes him. He is somehow threatened by her but I don't know why.

She sticks out her tongue at him and he responds by making scary faces until she shrieks. If she throws a bit of a tantrum, he reprimands her loudly although I try to impress upon him that she is only four and has limited self-control.

December 9, 2005

I wonder how many times I can listen to *Take My Breath Away* (Twenty-five times in three days, and play the game *Free Cell* hundreds of times) before I decide to have some different life.

I do need to call Dr. Gillette to find out if there is sometimes a sudden downturn—a break—or if will be a continual slow slide.

(Wow. Do I want a break, a quick snap? Dylan is singing about breaking just like a little girl. If Dave were to break, would it be a break for me? Do I wish for it?)

It is true: I think often about being free. But to wish another harm for my benefit is beyond the pale.

It continues to be so awful but fascinating at the same time. It is almost unbelievable. Just now while I was in the kitchen, making a drink and dinner decisions, Dave came in to say he wanted to clean up the 'stuff' on the table. I had to supply the answer to what the 'stuff' was, had not asked him because I guessed he would not know. It is the peanut hulls from our snack while watching CSI. I gave him a container and a paper towel to clean them up. Too late—he forgot why he wanted them.

It is 6:15…and what a bore. Shabbat no less. What happened to those good evenings with the girls, my first born, lovely Kathy, her partner Roxy? Always good food, a special meal and after the blessings, Simone tossing off the Challah cover with a *TA-DA*—she started that when only a baby.

Simone is so like Kathy, not only in their beauty but their willingness to charge into the world unafraid. Kathy had a hard time playing tennis because she had a tendency to drive the ball over the fence and into the hills. Simone never saw a mud puddle too wide to jump over, nor too deep to jump in.

Sad eyed lady of the lowlands, where the prophets say that no man comes. This is what Dylan sings now. *Should I put them by your gate?* Never mind the prophets, please put back the man I married.

༄

Winged Angels
As promised,
By our gate appeared.
Too late —
Earlier
TIME came
To take him
Assisted by laughing imps.

But stay, stay
Winged angels
Wait for me.

༄

 The chicken feed. He made three trips in three days up to Rainey's. Still no chicken feed, which is what he went for. Always ice cream and chips. Finally, today the cans of dog food, but no cans of cat food. Yes, however, to a bag of dry cat food.
 Is it right to ask of him? Why does *he* have to do it? Should he even be driving? Why not me? I can do only a few *out of the compound trips* a week. Yesterday I took Mazie to the Vet. Kathy picked her up, bless her.
 Today, the library. I would rather feed the chickens the more expensive sunflower seed meant for the birds than trade going to the library for the feed store.
 Oh, and the coffee. Today was worse than usual he was constantly making another cup, does not even notice the one cup at hand. Constantly micro-warming a found one, constantly re-heating water for a new one. *Too strong, too weak, too cold, too boiling over.*

Hey, I am trying to work here. I am already late getting my work to the printer. Stop with the coffee!

December 10, 2005

I'm seeing a crash and don't much like it. I cannot imagine a year of this. But, of course, it is winter.

Dark days.

◦◦

Earlier Times

I remember with clarity his confusion a day in January, 1996. I was irritated and tense that he would not move along at my speed. We were already late for the plane to Palm Springs for the celebration of my aunt and uncle's fiftieth wedding anniversary—I was their flower girl and remember parts of that of day also.

He stood in front of the buffet staring at the list of instructions for my niece who was caring for the animals in our absence. He moved the paper a few inches to the right, then to the left as though there were a perfect place for it and no other would do.

We were living an idyllic life on this sheep farm we began creating fourteen years before. We expected to stay forever. Bit by bit something started coming apart.

In June we headed for Eugene as usual for *The Black Sheep Gathering*, at that time, the only show in the US devoted to the raising of colored sheep for the development of special wool for hand spinners and weavers.

Dave and I had been in charge of the trade show for several years. Our first responsibility was laying out the booths in the barn. Not simple, but not difficult either.

This year Dave was unable to distinguish the dimensions of the aisles from the dimensions of the booths. We argued.

He: "I have been measuring spaces for years."

I: "But you haven't left room for aisles."

I remember becoming confounded by his obstinacy in the face of the clear error of measurement.

A laughing announcement went out: "Stay away from the Trade Show Barn until Dave and Michelle get it together. It could be dangerous."

It was funny at the time.

Chapter 2

When he first kissed me with a mouth that meant more than friendship, I knew the music had begun.

We were married in a wooden chapel on a hot summer day in 1976.

My daughters, Kathy and Jennifer, stood next to me.

Standing next to Dave, my son Patrick.

Dave took to his role as step-father with ease. Our families had been friends so he has known my children since they were very young, Jennifer and Patrick as babies. All children loved Dave—he respected them, listened to them, played with them and made them laugh with silly jokes.

We were a family in a way I had never experienced. We were involved in each others lives. We ate dinner together almost every night. The nights we didn't were called, *It's a Make Your Own Night*.

Several nights a week we congregated in the living room to listen to music and talk. Occasionally we were treated to a performance, usually musical; especially funny and entertaining was Patrick's rendition of Paul Simon's *Fifty Ways to Leave Your Lover*.

We never missed one of their school performances. They all were in Drama Class; Patrick played the trumpet in Band and Orchestra, Jennifer was a cheerleader.

We went camping, to Griffith Park and Olvera Street, museums and art galleries, a couple of afternoons to jazz venues, each year Renaissance Faire and sometimes one or the other would come with us when we sailed our sloop in Santa Monica Bay.

My family married a good man. Never was the promise not met. Never was there a time we were not speaking the same language.

Until later.

༄

Remember

Deliver yourself to me my love,
In full face, or in profile
With your history, or without
I ask not that from you, my love.

Walk with me, or not,
Lie with me, or claim another.
Keep me in your heart
And remember my name

༄

December 11, 2005

I do not see a 'disease,' but actions and consequences. It is so hard to accept that his motivation is often unfathomable to either of us. If I ask, "Why did you put the stamp over the address?" he does not know.

Even worse, "Why did you put water in my jewelry box?" He answered, equally puzzled, "I didn't, just thought you should see it."

When the 'todays' are too weighty, I will retreat into memories of 'yesterday.'

I am just going to put it down for myself, print it out every once in a while and read it like a book, maybe as though it is someone else's life, even though it seems so familiar.

My children will want to read it.

I was disappointed when I leafed through my father's journal, mostly political observations: decrying the potential loss of the middle class because of the welfare state...etc, etc.

I was hoping for something more personal. Maybe it is there. Will read more, and between the lines. He hated his parents; maybe there will be some of that.

I do not want *my* children to guess.

I am trying to find the soundtrack for tonight's writing, have on *Nessun Dorma*, Jussi Bjorling singing. But am impelled to go back to Dylan. (Okay just a few more minutes of this, and then the *Pearl Fishers*, then Dylan.)

1966 or so, my sister Kathy brought this singer to me. I thought Dylan's was the worst voice I had ever heard. Then a few years later, Neil Young... *Surely there was something wrong with the recording.*

Well what did I know, a lawyer's wife in a big house in Pasadena? During most of the fourteen years of my first marriage, I thought my path in life was set for adulthood and no longer included *Rock and Roll.* Hah!

I already embraced Joan Baez. So she and these other two are the soundtracks of the then and the now.

Over and over: *Trying to get to Heaven before they close the door.*

Heaven for me now would be to awaken to a bright June morning and prepare for our trip up the highway to *The Black Sheep Gathering*.

Dave and I would be in the ring with our best ewe, Black Magic, as we were fifteen years ago. We stood in first position, but the judge, after placing us, looked unsure. Dave and I worked to follow his instructions, "Get her rear legs set up right or I'll have to move her to second place." The sheep was resistant so we moved down a peg.

As we were leaving the ring with our red ribbon, Dave looked at the judge and said, "You're history in this town, man." Everyone cracked up – they all loved Dave – and the judge continued to tell the story years afterward.

December 12, 2005

The soundtrack tonight is Air Supply, *Old Habits Die Hard*. No, that doesn't quite work. Let's do *Sweet Dreams Are Made of This*.

Music is such a strong common thread for us, I the listener, he the player.

I am thinking of the night of the band party at our house, the San Marino house, soon after Dave and I became lovers.

The band—Dave and his friends—set up in front of the big window and just blew it out. Some neighbors and many kids came in to hear the jam. Dave has the most perfect tone and timing of anyone since Miles.

It must have been around Christmas, we had given Jennifer a little organ.

After everyone had left, Dave sat at this tiny organ and played to me. *Funny Valentine*.

༺༻

He and I started dating the holiday season of 1975. Dave's wife had gone off with their friend George two years before.

My children's father, Thomas, had left, bitter and self-righteous. Probably the best moment of my life was when he said I could have custody of the children. The year before he left had been frightening. He was so powerful... I was reduced to quaking. My nightmares ended after he died six or seven years ago. Maybe ten.

Our daughter Jennifer said, when hearing of his death, "I felt as though someone were telling me of the death of a stranger."

She still burns a *yertzeit* candle for him, however—on the anniversary of his death.

December 13, 2005

Oh what a nice day. Up early after a dream—Dave and I connected by an elastic tape with those little metal grippers on either end clamped to our t-shirt collars. No Freud needed here.

Once again, he found a short sleeve t-shirt, must have been rummaging in my closet where I had hidden them. *It is too cold, too cold.* But of course, he does not know that, it is warm for him here now. That the next moments, let alone the next hour, will be different from the present is something he can no longer grasp.

Yesterday he said he did not like the turtlenecks because they were too hard to get off the hangars. Today he said they were too confining and sweaty. Little clues I must use to form the whole of what he needs. How nice, how simple. Another solution to conflicts. Just get the facts ma'am. Give him only those long sleeve shirts with no collars…and get more.

And so, Ms. Montgomery, what is it you do with your time each day? Well, you know, this and that.

Yesterday I planted some pansies due to be set free from their containers. Fed the sheep and llamas… and cats and dogs…and chickens…and birds. Oh, myself and my husband.

Built Lego cities with Simone (actually, she built them; I was there at her request.) And we made a puppet show about the wizard turning the frog into a princess. There is probably a point to these children's myths so I go along.

And a crossword puzzle. And a bit of reading *Jonathan Strange and Mr. Norrell*.

Later, a long rich conversation with my friend Anne. Oh, do I miss seeing her every week. Last year we co-taught the kindergarten class at our Synagogue. Our friendship was sealed by our shared energy and resulting exhaustion engendered by a group of bright and rebellious five and six year-olds. Since then, I have become a recluse. Hearing from friends who still live in the world I used to, the easy sane one, is comforting.

And you feel guilty about not doing enough...because?

No place for guilt here; I will grow in my own way, at my own speed, to become the support that keeps us both from collapsing.

December 14, 2005

We are partial to the Italians, particularly DeNiro and Pacino. Also, Dustin is pretty amazing. Dave can still name them.

Tonight we watched another of our favorites, *The Bird Cage*. He instantly said, *Oh Robin*. We have seen it five or six times.

He got it, laughed. But only partly. When it was over, we stay for the credits, I asked him if he had ever seen this movie before. He said no.

He had a favorite movie when we were dating. Most everything we did involved our kids. We all went to Santa Monica to see *Armacord*.

So, I am sitting between my lover and my eleven year old son during this scene involving a young boy and a woman with huge naked breasts who is saying "Suck, don't blow."

I think it was one of the freakier moments of my life. We then went out for spaghetti. I drank a lot of wine. No mention of the movie.

December 15, 2005

I listen to this song often lately for these writing moments: *Girl you'll be a Woman Soon*, first Neil Diamond, then Urge Overkill.

Perhaps because my years of playing, laughing with life, are over—I am fully adult now.

What want to write is: Dave's spinning everything to the positive. You would think this would be right up my alley, being an idealist and optimist. However, I abhor opinions not informed by fact, perceptions that do not correspond to reality. My reality, of course.

The coyotes just now were howling. He said, "They are closer than usual." In the first place we have not heard them for many weeks. In the second place, they are not close at all.

I am suddenly grumpy at the end of a perfect day. The grumpiness probably has more to do with the movie we just saw than with Dave's misperception.

Crash, way too intense for me now. About bigotry and irony. Bigotry is poison, even seeing it is poisonous. The irony saved it from being completely toxic.

Before that, the perfect day:

It is misty, foggy, here in Sam's Valley during the winter. But sometimes the fog goes away, the sky clears, the temperature drops. I wake up in the morning to see these little sparkling jewels on the screen in my bathroom.

And the sun is out. And even though it still only 20 degrees, I can go out. Crunching in the hoarfrost is so much better than sloshing in the mud (which I admit has its attractions.)

I decided in this perfection, to take the day off. Did the feeding early. Started the turkey stock for the smell of it.

First fire of the year. And more of *Jonathan Strange and Mr. Norrell*.

DECEMBER 16, 2005

Kathy called around five asking if she and Simone could come over. *Of course.*

Her partner Roxy, another daughter for me, is in bad shape. The meds do not seem to keep her manic-depression under control. Their relationship is so full of conflicts. Rox cannot handle any stress— Kathy cannot handle an adult dependent. She will go to stay with her brother in Colorado for a while. A relief for us all; we all need a breather from the intensity.

Kathy and I are beginning to be concerned about Simone's being indulged. Neither Kathy, Roxy nor I seem to be able to say *no* to her. She's four and a half and a charming tyrant. We cannot have a conversation without her interrupting, trying to engage us in play.

So, I take the peanuts-in-shells we are munching and rain them on her, as she rained coins on me the other day. Her joy is an endorphin burst for me.

We do not know what to do about our own joy in hers, our indulging her for our own great pleasure and amusement. Will it mean she will grab life only for herself? Or will our caring teach her to care?

Kathy said, "In this society there is little regard for duty, obligations. We give lip service (duty to country, etc) but that is almost the antithesis of what most think it means to be American, which is all about freedom without constraints, freedom to do what we want. So duty, commitment to spouse, family goes by the wayside."

Me: "So we don't want to constrain our children either."

To quote Simone, "Oh pickles."

Our neighbor Pete was over the other day, asking about cutting some of our fallen trees, we asked him for his referrals about strong young kids to help with various farm and garden chores. He is a nice guy, they are good neighbors.

Then he asked if our cats wandered. They had cats coming around they did not want.

I said, "No, our two cats stay here."

He said, "Okay, then I can shoot those stray cats."

I was repelled. "Why?"

"They're just cats."

As long as I live, I will never understand this mentality.

My life is with a man who can barely swat a fly. Years ago we had two ewes who became so lame they could only get about on their knees. At the point when I could no longer bear their suffering, I asked Dave to shoot them. We usually call the livestock slaughterer for this chore, but we were short of money. He did it but was very shaken and implored, "Please don't ever ask me to do that again."

Whatever had I been thinking?

Chapter 3

Dark Blue Bathrobe

You take your dark blue bathrobe off the hook,
A long ago gift from Katie and Patrick.
You find the place for your arms,
The sash eludes you
I help tie it

You wear it
And wear it... in the day
In the night... to bed... to the garden
When company comes... or when strangers
Your security blanket, your momma and bubbe.

DECEMBER 17, 2005

Kathy and Simone were here for a while. Kathy brought groceries: my grapefruits, turkey bacon, and chicken breasts, which we cannot get at Rainey's, that little country store three miles up the road, is just about as far as I am willing to go these days. It takes all my energy to focus on my new role: Caregiver.

I'm beginning to see some of his thought processes. It helps my moving beyond irritation, annoyance. He was watching *Law and Order.* TV land, where he feels safe yet busy. After Kathy and Simone left, I came here to my office to write. In a minute, the dogs outside started barking. Dave came in, alarmed, said, "Oh, I didn't know anyone was here. Heard the dogs barking…"

After he went back to the living room, I was curious, went to ask, "Didn't you know I was in my office? You seemed surprised to see me."

He said, "Yes, I was, you were lower. I expected you higher on the stage."

I am back in my office, sitting down now, as I was when he came in. It is over, the astonishment at his dementia. Scorning it, I cast shock away. I accept the madness: it is here. I will become its student. My favored role.

All the jewelry ads on TV for the holidays remind me of the day we went to buy our wedding rings. JC Penney's in the Arcadia Mall. Found just what I wanted. The smallest sliver of a gold band. $14.00.

I have not taken it off since June 26, 1976. Is that trippy or what, almost thirty years of a bind/bond? And this for a woman who gets claustrophobic.

Some things are just worth it.

DECEMBER 18, 2005

I am becoming so addicted to the evolution of this story I come in earlier and earlier to write. Cannot believe I am giving up James Lipton's interview of Barbara Walters, though I will run back and forth, have already.

Well, will have to come back to this. Can't miss it—she is really wonderful. One of the last questions Lipton always asks is, "What profession other than your own would you like to have?" She said, "Teacher, but it is far down the list from what I am doing." When looks at her interview, she will no doubt see how much a teacher she is—such a noble calling and one I aspire to.

I am trying to figure out what this writing is. For me alone? For my kids and grandkids? For someone who is doing an historical analysis of sixty-two-year-olds at the beginning of the 21st century?

For those who are listening now?

I hope to be a teacher in this, to help those going through it also. To say, *it's not so bad, not so bad.* Keep your place, keep your humor, listen, above all listen to your own voice, to his, to those who care.

I need to read May Sarton again. See what she captured in her journals. How she managed to make her ordinary life seem worthy of being read about and it was. Something in the pictures she paints and her deep reactions to circumstances.

And Virginia Wolfe. Her loneliness and despair overwhelmed her at times, as I sometimes feel overwhelmed. So she wrote. I write to take it out and look at it, a puzzle to be solved, conquered really.

Today. Each day I set goals. Awake with them. Sometimes it is a little bit light through the blinds, often dark. As I roll over, pulling the pillows back over my head, or pushing them away, I think of coffee and the first cigarette…and the goals. What the day is about. Is it raining, freezing, sun? I have no preference.

And always, the *Modah Anee*, my Hebrew prayer of awakening again, whispered, often sung out. Ah ha! Alive again. Another day!

Today the major goal was the holiday fudge.

Seemed as though I was wading through fudge itself to get to the chore.

I have a dear old aunt, and a dear cousin in Seattle. A dear cousin in Palm Springs. Fudge for the last 20 years has been my gift. This was a project Dave and I loved.

Put on some wonderful music, smoke a joint, and mushy up the stuff. How can he not remember that? Today, it was the forgetting again.

I decided to do the first batch myself. Not so good. Hard to stir and add the chocolate and marshmallow alone. (Where the hell is my third hand?)

Second batch. I to him: Drizzle the chocolate around the edges, not in the middle." Of course, it goes in the middle. Last in first out. I need to learn to convey only one direction at a time.

"Will you stir, my arm and hand are tired? Vigorously, while it is still hot."

He is such a gentle man he cannot even stir fudge with vigor. Does he think stirring will hurt it?

Holding a sheep as required for medicating is nothing he could ever do well. That their future well-being required it was not something he could see. Stressing the struggling beast *now* is what worries him.

December 19, 2005

Where's Gramma, I want to see my Gramma.
The dream:
Simone is screaming at my memorial service at the Havurah.
Those who were not crying before are crying now.
In awareness of incomprehensible loss.

What a horrible dream, afraid it was prophetic. I thought nightmares had stopped after my first husband, the subtle abuser, died. And they did those dreams. These are new ones.

Kathy was here for a few hours. Grieving, finally beginning to accept her loved one is lost to her. She is accepting Roxy cannot be her partner. Rox's multiple ailments, her bi-polar, her ADD, her fibromyalgia.

In sickness and in health? But what of the child? What of Simone? Doesn't she need both mothers? What is asked of us, truly?

I sorrow for my daughters, my 38 year old baby, lovely Jennifer, is also in pain. Another marriage falling apart.

These are the things that sadden me now; I do not grieve for myself or Dave any longer, there is too much funny stuff going on:

Yesterday, he came to me with sweat pants on, but no shirt, asking if I had seen his tee shirts. I admitted I had hidden them. He would be better off with the long sleeve shirts. He was okay with it, he is letting me take care of him.

This morning he dressed in a long sleeve turtleneck and his bathrobe.

I directed him to his sweat pants. Led him, actually, sat him down and proceeded to pull the pant legs over his feet and up his legs. He chuckled and said, "This better be good."

December 20, 2005

Awoke this morning recalling, another disturbing dream.

Dave was dressed in his bathrobe, a shirt opened down his chest, and a pink sweater of Simone's stretched across. He left the house for a while, came back with a down comforter which cost $89.40. I was angry because we have lots of down comforters, and I am trying not to spend money from our thin budget on non-necessities.

I was also angry because he had ruined Simone's sweater by stretching it out.

He left by the front gate and came back with the information that he had been diagnosed with rheumatoid arthritis rather than Alzheimer's.

I raged that I would lock the gate so he could not leave.

Earlier Times

Our transition from city dwellers to country folk was seamless. We had no attachment to our Arcadia house which I bought after my divorce. The only nice feature was the back yard we paved in brick to make a lovely fern garden under a huge shade tree. The house itself was a pieced together bit of ugly, all I could afford.

It is true we generated many, many happy memories there as a family—when the time came, we simply packed up the memories and took them with us. As the kids grew up and headed for college, the traffic and the smog continued to choke us; we saw no reason to stay.

In our carefree embrace of life we didn't worry that we had no jobs waiting as we planned our move to Oregon where my sister and her large family lived. As a musician Dave was a true free-spirited artist. I was attending college full time soaking up the air of the rebellious seventies.

Our shared love of animals drew us to the 'back to the land' movement of the time. Dave brought armloads of books from the library on homesteading, livestock husbandry, and organic vegetable gardening.

We packed up and left town the day after our younger daughter Jennifer's high school graduation. We drove off with a whoop without a backward glance or regret. After renting for three months in the town of Ashland, home of artists, hippies and the annual Shakespeare Festival, we found our dream: thirty acres of pasture bordered by a creek and a one third mile long stand of trees along the driveway—oaks, ash, and pine. And a house that had a roof and a bathroom, our only real requirements. Lucky for us it also had three bedrooms, living room, and kitchen.

Chapter 4

DECEMBER 21, 2005

We just watched the most frightening movie I have ever seen, *Mysterious Skin*. It's a story of two boys who were sexually abused by a trusted baseball coach when they were eight.

One of these days I will write in this diary about the abuse our step father rained on my sister, brother and me (my younger brother claims he probably deserved any harsh treatment he received from his natural father; younger sister apparently was left alone.) One does not have to be raped to feel raped. I was relieved when that man died last year. Good riddance.

I don't do well at Yom Kippur. I accept I don't have to forgive those who have no remorse, but still, I would like to be able to for me. Hate and revulsion are poisons.

When my mother was dying, I wanted to tell her how badly she served us, did not protect us, did not do her duty. Instead, I told her I loved her. I think that was not true, not entirely anyway. I am sorry for her. She chose that man rather than her children.

I will probably write about how he liked to massage his children before they went to bed. I will probably write about the night he asked if I wanted to have my breasts massaged. I was fifteen. I said no, though it was difficult. He had all the power, but he backed off.

I will probably write about the time he gave me a book he claimed to have written about his love affair with a woman in Italy during the war. He was in the war, but why did he give me this book? Why did he want me to know of his sexual escapades? Now I doubt he wrote it but used it as an excuse for some game he alone knew the rules to or for some perverted fantasy.

I will probably write of the time he, just out of the shower walked by me with an erection. He could have easily claimed he did not know I was there. And perhaps also write of the time he gave me information on birth control while mother was out of the house. In all the uncomfortable details of methods before there was a 'pill.'

He said a neighbor looking through the window had caught me with my lover, Lauren. He relished describing our activity, ostensibly to prove the truth of what the neighbor had told him.

Mother was never there for any of this. I wish I had been able to tell her. Was I afraid or embarrassed? Afraid of him, the denials and repercussions; embarrassed with my mother: we never talked of sex.

Yes, some day I will write about it.

December 22, 2005

I don't feel like writing tonight. That movie last night really unnerved me, I was tense all day. I can't imagine how children survive real physical abuse. My step-father abused me by innuendo; still, all this time later, it is hard to deal with. *I must let go.*

My rambling thoughts have no anchor so I do need to get back to the diary, come back into this *present* life. I need somehow to separate out the memories not directly related to *the now*.

Maybe I need a separate diary, a diary of old memories if I can't leave them alone, including a separate section for bad memories. I am not sure I want my children to read them and feel regret for me.

Maybe if I had known some of the depth of my mother's life, not just the good things, I would have been more able (or be more able) to understand. In our extended family, the bad things were stuck in the closet. I might accept what was perhaps her need to protect and take care of herself before her children.

Soon after our parents' divorce she moved us to Palm Springs and its buzzing social life— social life for adults. We were well provided for, but having enough to eat, clothes to wear does not constitute nurturing.

I really don't get, no matter how I search, how she could have told me to drown those mice, call the animal control men take my cats, and then drive away, off to a pool party no doubt. I was ten. (Of course, I did not drown the mice they went back in the golf bag where they would be found by their mother.)

Ten years old. Those two days are among my most indelible memories. I was such a good girl, rarely disobeyed my mother. Even to talk or to argue would have been unthinkable.

Kathy, Roxy, and I are making sure Simone is not a 'good' girl. *Shout it out if you are being hurt! If you do not want me to kiss you, I will not. Shout it out.*

Now, I will be able to catch up on the diary. That long ago is gone for now.

I have this other idea.

Today while doing our mailings, we listened to Paul Simon. *Still Crazy After All These Years* was our song, one from the soundtrack of the early days of our marriage.

We had so many crazy family evenings. Patrick could do a fun and funny miming of that song, complete with the fake mike. We liked sitting around together, the whole family. Thinking back now, it seems weird; Dave and I drank and smoked. How could the kids stand being there in all the smoke? Must have been worth it to them. I will ask this weekend when we are in Eugene.

Music all the time. Ours, but mainly theirs: Eagles, SuperTramp, Patti Smith, Cars, Joan Armatrading... And the trans generational: Joan Baez, Beatles, Stones, Dylan, NeilYoung, Paul Simon, Donovan. Their friends loved to come over. Patrick's best friend, Bobby, and Kathy's best friend, Jill aka Harriet Storm, called me Mom. Dave was everyone's favorite dad—so childlike and full of fun himself.

There have been times in my life when it is so perfect, I think, *Ok, I can die now.*

Oh, back to my idea. Feed off a particular lyric line(s), see where it goes. This today, from Paul Simon: *And I don't know a soul who's not been battered*

Many of my adult friends have been psychologically battered by their parents. We come from a strange generation, the generation of all powerful adults, children are to be seen and not heard; just wait until your father gets home; do you want your mouth washed out with soap?

Ah, the poets. Just catch it right, often.

It seems I did want to write tonight. It's like gardening, once you pull the first weed, you're committed – works every time.

December 25, 2005

Back in my cave again. How nice. I am very, very tired after the trip to Eugene yesterday for Xmas eve and Xmas morning. Since I converted to Judaism, Christmas means nothing to me other than family, so it's worth it, but my shoulder muscles are so tight from dealing with my emotions. I am way too inner focused, must get out of myself and go out again into the lives of others.

The highlight:

A deeply gratifying conversation with my two oldest grand sons, Alex, 13 and Grant, 11. They are sharp kids and used to solving problems, so we talked about ethics. One of the basic tenets of Judaism is that actions and consequences are more important than intentions. I posed this as a question for the boys: "Is intention or result the determinant of the 'goodness' of one's actions?" It was a lively discussion, much to my delight.

I believe morality and ethics can be (or are) taught, but suspect the inclination toward good comes from the parental nurturing and example.

They clearly understood the question, but wanted to answer it in terms of who would be punished. Alex felt the evil person who did a bad act that resulted in good was still evil, but should not be punished. Grant felt someone who was good but did something bad, *should* be punished.

Both felt intention was important, but we did not get to the tertiary level: accidental harm, whether the good person who lapsed for one act could still be considered good, how many good acts with good intention would an evil person have to do to graduate to the *good* side? The possibilities for discussion are endless – I am sure we will have many more of them.

I had a bit of difficulty coming up with real life possibilities. Initially, each felt there could be no such scenario. Accidental harm is the easiest: Oppenheimer's participation in developing nuclear power comes to mind. My understanding is it plagued him too.

No doubt, this is what God meant by providing free will. Apparently, angels do not have these discussions. Neither do they have these terrific kids.

DECEMBER 26, 2005

He is driving me crazy letting the animals in and out. I thought *I* was empathic. Forget it. Nothing compared to his worrying about how cold they might be. If they are hungry, thirsty, need attention, too tall, too short, too dog-like, too cat-like.

I'm beginning to see the possibility of projection in his concerns. Maybe mine too. Our concern for others mirrors our concern for ourselves.

Case in point: a friend visited this weekend; we discussed several unknown species of spiders in her house, most dead. I felt sorry for them and made a face.

She said, "Well, they're just spiders."

Wow, do I hate that. Nothing alive is *just*.

December 27, 2005

I haven't read any of this yet, except to go back to the prior day to see if I have been foolish.

Did I write about the day last week when I was walking down the creek path to feed the sheep and llamas in barn four? About ten, maybe twenty feet, probably twenty, through the creek gate, I noticed splatted white bird droppings beneath the big oak. (Not the big tree that dropped down dead a month ago, but a big tree nonetheless.)

Anyhow, I looked up, suspecting, hoping really I would see the dropper. Indeed. The smallest falcon I had ever seen. Not more than six, maybe eight inches. Scoped the wing span as he (she?) flew off, not more than twelve inches. Came back to look in Fielding's Guide. No such falcon. Brought the query to Patrick this Xmas weekend.

He asked, "Could it have been a kestrel?" Indeed. God I love that kid. What an amazing mother I must be to have these amazing children.

December 28, 2005

Once again, I feel as though I can barely write. This seems to be the norm these evenings when it gets dark so early. Or perhaps I am depressed.

Tammy, my dear sweet niece was here today. Last February she attempted suicide. Through the most unlikely chain of events, she was rescued. Sometimes we are forced so close to the edge only a miracle can save us. She was on the *brink* where disastrous life-changing decisions are made.

Once I was driving through the civic center, the kids in the back, having survived another nasty session with the cult therapist Thomas insisted on. David Bowie was singing, *Changes… Ch, ch, ch, changes.*

At that moment I thought it was a good day to die. Die with personal power. Choose your moment. Die happy…if possible, with no regrets, not when you are forced to the edge of a cliff. Only years later did I hear my thought as lyrics in a Robbie Robertson song titled with those words: *It's a Good Day to Die.*

At that time I was contemplating *changes,* frightening changes. That moment was happy with my realization that the *changes* would be a good thing. The contemplation of escape from my power monger husband, from the woman who empowered him to be a dominator for her own reasons, consolidating her power, and gathering his money, his obeisance.

My Dave is so much stronger. He went to the same woman to save his marriage. That woman was better at destroying marriages. Dave turned in his keys and empowered me to turn in mine. We were kindred spirits. He always knew bullshit when he saw it…I had to learn. Much later. He taught me—teaches me still about a life well lived.

DECEMBER 29, 2005

When Tammy walked in the door yesterday I could not believe how beautiful and alive she looked. She had downed more pills than one can and live.

She was part of a chat room. She said something that alerted one of the others. None had met. This person did a search, called the police who found the address and came to save her.

Connections, connections will save us.

This child Tammy was one of the saved out of that family. Her father is my brother, Chip, Victor Montgomery III.

This is so hard to write, this horrible memory:

My little brother, Chip, was only a baby in his crib. I was in my bed, pretending to be asleep. Because he was a baby, did not know how to pretend, he was holding onto the rail, bouncing high. Our father came in and spanked him for not sleeping. I remember this as though it were yesterday. I want to throw up.

When we moved to Palm Springs, Mother was young, thirty-two, beautiful, and liked parties. We were often left with our housekeeper, Emily, Black-Cherokee, who believed there were little red spiders in the core of lettuce that would do something or other to you; that earwigs would climb in your ears and go into your brain.

When seven years old Chip was found hitchhiking home after leaving school in the middle of the day. He was sent off to Black Fox Military School because he was too hard for Mother to handle. He was seven years old for God's sake, what were they thinking?

To help her share the burden Mother married a monster who could not tolerate the slightest disobedience or lapse. He was especially infuriated by dirty finger nails, so he scoured Chip's until they were bright pink, just a tad from bloody. Many other infractions got him spanked with a belt. But even he couldn't cope with my sweet brother being nothing more than a boy-child, so off again to boarding school.

I am overwhelmed with sadness. The horrible trail. What kind of a marriage, a family, was he expected to have after such a childhood? First a harsh father, then an even harsher step-father. One of his sons is perpetually in prison; the other often lives homeless under bridges.

We thought Tammy was the survivor. Indeed, now she is, but precarious? I hope not. I see now my brother is a survivor too. But what will become of those nephews of mine?

Chapter 5

JANUARY 3, 2006

We may have gotten through something. Very big for me, big for me because I assume it is for him.

Yesterday Simone and I made brownies. We didn't have an egg, so used extra oil. They turned out gooey and rich on the inside, too crispy on the outside. Simone commented on this specifically, ate part of one but had no interest in taking any home. When they turn out well, she eats several.

Today while stamping postcards, Dave was munching on his third or fourth. This is the part I always hate: I took away the half-eaten one and said they were not good for his intestinal workings.

He said, "I haven't had that problem in a long time."

I bristled slightly and said, "No, that is not the case, I spent an hour two days ago washing your bedding."

I went back to my office feeling lousy. I hate taking choices away from him; hate the possibility he feels humiliated.

When I came back through, he said, "You know, you are right, I have been eating this candy, soft and hard parts, brown stuff dripping off my face. I won't do it anymore. I'll just eat bananas."

He loves bananas. He thanked me for pointing this out, for watching out for him. What a relief. A relief, apparently, he does not feel humiliated by my taking care of him.

I woke up this morning feeling wonderful. My tension lessened for the moment, the tension of having such power and the tension of being out here alone and having my old dear Buick as my only exit. Oh yeah, it was a good start to the day. And this resolution of ours was not frosting on the cake. Instead, the bottom layer.

When I listened to Dylan singing this I thought: *it might reflect my dark side, the side that often would rather not be here—But it ain't me, babe... I'm not the one you need.*

But no, no dark side: *it is me, babe.* I will be here for you. I am sure of this.

My former husband, Thomas, enjoyed humiliating me. It may have been to reclaim potency he didn't otherwise have. I want never to do that to someone I love. How would I have cared for him under these same circumstances? Repay his abuses in kind or take the high road? I am guessing I would pity him, though for Dave I have only loving compassion, not pity.

The truth is, I am a bit afraid of men, intimidated by their power. But I am reluctant to write of it because of my son Patrick – afraid he will think I look at him differently than I do his sisters. Of course I love them all equally and am not at all intimidated by him.

Children, even grown ones, are easily crushed by parents. That core child is always there. I am just a little girl deep down. All I have are lace panties with bells on them, blue velvet dress with a lace collar, patent leather Mary Janes. I do as the grown-ups tell me.

But I fooled them. They did not realize they could not control me once I went to school...or not entirely anyway. I went to first grade and learned the word: *Jump!* The beginning of personal power: I can read!

Hah, I *really fooled* them. There *is* a *me* in here – not a plaything, not a subservient: an independent free person. Gotcha!

January 4, 2006

Kathy came today with a possible solution to the impasse between Simone and Dave. The impasse had been ongoing for the last year. Perhaps it is jealousy – each of them jealous of the attention I give the other.

Simone came in, charged up, saying, "Where is Grandpa?"

Grandpa was in bed, first nap of the morning.

She bolted into his room and said, "It's a nice day."

We now have a chart on which we put a smiley face every time she is nice to Grandpa. At the end of seven smiley faces, she gets a set of *Bobble Heads*. When she was disinclined to say, "Thank you" for his proffered chips, I suggested this would be a chance to win another Smiley Face. She replied, "I only get one a day." I decided to change the rule to assure her ongoing compliance: "No, not the rule anymore, you can have as many as earned." Not surprisingly, the "Thank you" was forthcoming.

Kathy had explained to her we do not do this for the reward only, but because of what we have in our heart.

Simone: "My heart is not that big."

Oh, well, it will grow. For now, it will be the reward and the habit.

Educating Dave was next, so we all practiced being nice to each other, manners. She is really trying, but he cannot resist making faces at her. It scares her. Scares me sometimes.

Later, the second time she was here today, she complained, "Grandpa is watching 'my' show." It was *Stuart Little*. After it was over, Dave said, "Interesting show." One look from me halts a mean response from my wild child. Dave 76, Simone 4; they are almost the same age now. I have to admit, I was also focused on the story. The cat was scary.

All day I was thinking how to take back from last night's writing that I was afraid of men. I know it is logically unfair to generalize. After all, I was hit only twice. Not by Dave. Many women would think being hit only twice is a gift. But then, I have also been attacked by my little boys, my grandsons. Enraged, not at me, the anger is just there. This testosterone is frightening.

Other boys blowing themselves up and as many others as they can. It makes me cry.

Every morning when Dave wakes up, he comes to me in my office with some funny shtick. For a long time it was a boxer stance and air punches. I hated it. Why would pretend hitting be funny? He never understood… or remembered.

What would be the ideal life for me now? My family near. A man back. One who has not forgotten the subtleties of irony. Who once again knows when I am being factious.

I grab at that, but it is not there. Will never be there. Not from him.

⁓

As you drift
I center.
One of us must
Cannot be you.

Whence comes this denouement?
The visible fading into
The ghost of nothingness
The pale of forgetting?

⁓

January 5, 2006

We are watching *Mr. Holland's Opus,* again. A wonderful story about ordinary people and their dreams, or their getting-bys. As movies must, it has a wonderful finale. We all write the pages toward our finales as we go along.

With this writing, I am becoming a sponge. When I started this I didn't think I had the writer's memory eye. That is less true now, not because of honing my eye, more from absorbing how others write, how the eyes and ears of other writers inform them. They are alert to their environment, internal as well as external.

I also have learned memories added to the story are not indulgences, but really the warp of the fabric. The structure upon which the weft of present experiences is woven into the whole of one's life fabric. Today, my memories and the present are very close in time. For the last three or so years I have been reclusive. Not because I didn't want social contact, but because of feeling insecure. I don't know what happened to me.

Whoa, hello, writing as therapy. *Of course!* It was three years ago Dave really started to lose it. Seven years ago his memory loss began, or was becoming evident. It was then I began to lose my rock, my anchor, the one who could and would always save me, the one I depended on to support me if I faltered, catch me if I fell. So now, the roads are more perilous, especially at night: no lights, no shoulders. Not having his shoulder to lean on is sometimes too painful to think about.

But today! It was *jump down pick a bale of cotton, jump down, pick a bale of hay.* I have my new little car. No worries, no breakdowns, no flat tires in the middle of nowhere.

Who would have thought all one needs to live is a vehicle? And of course, family, good friends, and the *kindness of strangers.*

The taste of spring is here. Yesterday, two bluebirds. I have their houses ready to put up. A quad of greedy female red-winged black birds is at the feeder, gobbling the suet, downing the sunflower seeds, arguing in mid-air contentions. Storing up the energy for breeding, nesting, egg laying, raising young. Then an hour later a young male, just yellow bars, no red yet, comes in. They feed here then go over to Kathy and Roxy's pond for nesting in the reeds. A wonderful mystery how they do all this.

The early snowdrops have been flowering for about a week. Daffodils seriously thrusting their green shoots.

I love the Winter Solstice because the day after I get to see all of this.

I love knowing more than I did yesterday.

Yesterday I learned a new word: polymath: a person learned in many fields.

January 7, 2006

"Have you ever made something like that?"

My God, it is practically the only thing I make: chicken marinated in soy, olive oil, garlic, and lemon juice, cooked in the micro. Rice with juniper berries and cardamom pods (added at the last minute). Sautéed carrots. Usually broccoli, though not tonight. Last night for Shabbat included wilted spinach salad with (turkey) bacon.

Ok, that's it. I am out of here. I have been such a good girl. Such a good person. Such a good Jew.

No more. I am going off to that place. That place in my head. The Children's Museum in Briarcliff four years ago where I saw that man. Just a glimpse of him across the room. He is the one I could now go to museums and concerts with. We would go to Paris again, as we would every year.

And as I did when Dave and I were there, I would laugh with the cab driver at my halting French while I congratulated him on

France's win at the world soccer tournament. He did not like us much until that stilted conversation. It is so easy to like another person.

That man and I will be mindless, those hard and foggy barriers thrown away, gone, we would be like rolling kittens.

Where shall I put my rage? I thought it was over. I am still fretting over his not remembering the chicken dish. I had this unrealistic fantasy things would get no worse. After all, there has not been much change for a while. Oh God, who am I fooling? I now make his lunches, sometimes help him dress. And undress when he goes to bed fully clothed with jacket and shoes. Remind him it was his sister who sent us the poinsettias.

I want to be Uma Thurman dancing with John Travolta. Meg Ryan falling in love again with Billy Crystal.

And Ilsa. Well, hell, I am Ilsa. How ironic. A woman in love with a man she cannot have, who is now lost to her, and tied to a man as her duty. Dave is both Rick and Victor Laszlo. My favorite movie, *Casablanca* comes back to haunt me.

I know so much, and so little about myself. What I do not know is how far I will go to survive.

Chapter 6

JANUARY 8, 2006

Well, today I made a mistake, maybe a huge one. Maybe not one at all, maybe part of the catharsis, the therapy. I downloaded three versions of *Unchained Melody*. They all made me cry. The Al Green version is the one I remember best. Ouch. Mega pain.

I keep saying this because it is true: *I do not want to be here anymore. I want to be back then.*

Oh my love, my darling, I hunger for your touch, I hunger for your love. Are you still mine?

This morning he paced a bit in the nude, looking for his underwear.

I directed him to the place they have always been. I wonder, *even if he has forgotten where it is, doesn't he see there is only one place in his room it could be?*

We did okay at the market, though I am sometimes frustrated by how much more time it takes when he is with me. I put raisins in the cart. Moments later he asks, "Don't we need raisins?" Perhaps my putting them there is what reminded him we needed them; he could not connect the two observations.

Well, of course, that's what the whole thing is about, lost connections; connections in his brain, connections between him and reality.

Good thing: when we sit at the table and put together the mailings, we always listen to music, a huge range, my choice, one of our connections.

I put on Chet Baker for him. He asked me who was playing (five years ago, no way, he knew even the most obscure, and of course Chet Baker is not obscure).

I told him. He said, "Far out, Chet Baker playing Miles." Indeed. That is just what he was doing. Yeah! The day he forgets Miles will be a sad one – perhaps even sadder than when he forgets me because it will mean even music is lost to him, a bit of emotional memory gone. Miles was his idol. He has many influences, but Miles was his main man in the world of jazz, the excitement, the freedom. Indeed, the freedom time in his life when he still made choices.

I prefer live jazz, seeing the musicians interact, work it out together perhaps the most interactive of genres. But even for me, Miles works anywhere; the living room is fine.

Dave has the Miles' tone, the same perfect timing. When I watched him (Dave, but of course Miles) play I was overcome by his perfection. And how much he loved it. A small group of people doing something that was almost pure, spirit the music flowing from heart, through head, to hand or mouth.

Dave has the heart of a comic. When he blows a note in his attempt to stretch, as all these guys do, he laughs; they all give some goofy response at those moments: "Forgot to eat your Wheaties this morning?"—the play of playing.

Patrick fixed up his trumpet and flugelhorn, honed the valves, oiled both, and sent along extra oil. I keep forgetting to bring them out. For him to play again would be so good.

This book I am reading, *The Run Away Bride*, explores two different kinds of love between a man and a woman. One is the falling in love, that non-thinking, the forever. This one never fails. The early passion continues in the core of all experiences of the beloveds together.

The other is the rational, the *this is what is good, what will work*. This one always fails.

I have had both kinds of love. The rational with Thomas. What could I have been thinking to marry with no passion? Being a perfect couple got *us* three perfect children, *me* pain and angst, and the kids much confusion. None of them felt sorry when he died, only regretted that things weren't different.

Ironic: he died of a brain tumor. He had no heart.

This one, this Dave of mine, will stretch me until I dissolve, explode, or am saved. Hey, any of it works for me. Dissolving or exploding would be my first choices. I suspect, however, I will be saved.

January 9, 2006

"Will you close the drapes, and I'll get dinner ready?"

"Which drapes, these drapes?" *Jeeze, no, the drapes at the National Gallery.* In all fairness, there are four sets of drapes in the room.

The difference between *the* drapes, and *this* drape might have eluded him. And why not? He has all these globbies and twists in his brain.

I have gotten close to that when trying to remember someone's name. Or the specifics of Kant's *categorical imperative*, especially why it is a logical necessity. Actually, I do remember that, but communicating it is something else. The balk between brain and mouth. The wishing we could just send our thoughts on air streams to the other. Only if we intend to, however. I would go to the grave before offering all my thoughts to whoever asked for them.

Dave/Simone parallels: A couple of days ago, Dave brought out a half-full can of cat food from the fridge. He asked if he should feed the cats. I said, "No, I give them their wet food in the morning. They always have their dry food in the garage. I feed the animals; you don't have to worry about it."

Well, not unexpectedly, the food was soon gone. Much to the delight of the cats. Oh well, they are old and will never be fat again.

He did it because he was going in that direction. Perseverating. Fixated, cannot change direction.

On the other end, Simone:

Wanting to take the toy school bus with little people home, she listened attentively and patiently to my explanation that, as with the little plastic wild animals, if they left here, they would probably not come back, in spite of her agreement they would. In which case, they would not be here to play with.

She absorbed my argument, then turned and walked out with the school bus. Her actions were exactly the same as Dave's, but her choice was....a choice.

(In fact, as she was leaving, she reconsidered and brought back the bus.)

Tonight, Dave tried to feed carrots to the rams. He forgets it is the llamas who like carrots, not the sheep. I saw him carefully setting something down on the back steps. I looked later. It was a pretty line of carrots. Except for Dempsey who sometimes jumps the fences into the garden, there is no one to eat these carrots.

When I see this, I want to say, as my grandmother would at such a thing, "God bless him." I picked up the carrots, washed them, ate one, and put them back into the fridge.

My grandmother was an extraordinary woman. My first memory of her was when she was visiting us at our house on Linden Drive. I was trying to write, and I asked her "How do you spell 'I'?" She said, "'I'," the letter 'I'."

What could be more simple? What better gift to give a child wanting to learn to read and write?

Soon after that, I went to Malibu Club, my grandfather's resort in Canada without my parents even though I was only five. We had our picture in the paper on the Society Page. Little me and these notable relatives.

We flew from Los Angeles to Seattle. Then Grandpa took us on his plane which I could help him drive, one of those that land on the water. I sat on his lap and helped him drive the plane.

While there I got polio, they think it was polio anyway. I was very sick. Grandma stayed with me all the time, reading me *Wind in the Willows*.

I was sent back home with Hannah, a servant, their cook, on a train. I liked Hannah. She was in our life for a long, long time. But I had to sleep in the train bed with her. Not so comfortable for me. She slept fine. I was little, five, after all. My parents met us at the beautiful big train station in LA.

The many times Dave and I went to Olvera Street, I would see that station and remember.

All I wanted was to be home with my little sister, Kathy. She was standing in the hall near our play room. My baby, I can remember the smell of her. Sort of like earth.

Who were these people in those days? They must have played and partied a lot. They were always leaving their children and possessions behind. I remember going with Daddy to retrieve something or other mother had left at a big house, one with a tennis court.

And then, to Macambo, the night club, to retrieve her gloves. I would not have been surprised to see Rick in the shadows by the palm fronds, Ilsa still at the table, Dooley Wilson at the piano. Good memories, I loved nothing better than being with my father.

∽

I had a Dream once
Of wearing my Mother's ball Gown
Full Skirt of white Lace, Bodice just so
Cap Sleeves over her Shoulders, lightly
Trimmed in black Lace.
And the Whisper of Arpège.

∽

Daddy and Dave got along wonderfully. The three of us were quite a group traveling in Europe together. Those are memories for another day. I am sad enough right now losing Dave. Remembering losing my father is more than I can deal with tonight.

Chapter 7

January 11, 2006

I want to chart Dave's ways of being in the world. I am guessing it will show a slow progress of the disease. Clues began to appear ten years ago, mostly not doing things I asked, or doing what I had asked him not to. I thought it was passive aggression.

But recording is tedious, so is done with morning energy, the time of day I also have the energy for dreaded housekeeping and other chores: checking the news, making the bed, seeing to the kitchen, the evening meal, if any. Making sure bills are paid, postcards sent, e-mails responded to. In the recent past, checking the market, making trades, or not. Feeding animals; laundry; our marketing work. My volunteer work overseeing the newsletter of my synagogue – that work is more time consuming now, because I am doing the formatting as well as the editing, *Damn power woman, no limits.*

And watching, forever watching over Dave. *I must drive him crazy with my attention.*

I have decided to check on myself to see whether the changes I want to make are in his interest, or because I want things to be *right*; right according to me.

How much does it matter if he makes a salad so big it lasts for days and rots before we finish it? Do I care that the salad after day four is not a good salad? No. I just want it to be done my way. It is as though I have certain inviolable rules and become annoyed when not followed.

But here again, I remind myself he is losing the ability to plan ahead, anticipate consequences. He cannot choose, I can.

Control freak. You are just like your mother. Let it go. Listen to love.

I want to do a bit of amateur psychology. Something I have been trying to figure out.

Why do Patrick and Katie have such a good marriage when Patrick's father was not a good role model in the waning days of our marriage? Am I the model for his choice of wife? Maybe. She is a dear one. A third daughter.

Why have the girls, Kathy and Jennifer, had such a hard time?

Jennifer marrying a man, a good man, who is so full of his own needs there is little room for her. Though more for their boys, *Baruch Hashem. Thank God.*

And Kathy, choosing, twice, partners not compatible enough for a life-time relationship. Is this a legacy of both parents?

January 12, 2006

After the usual office and housekeeping, I just lolled about, enjoying myself, reading a friend's novel manuscript. Immersing myself in fun; fun is…fun.

I keep asking the question of why I feel I must work to insure the happiness of others even though it sometimes means sacrificing a bit of my happiness. What I want for others is what I have. So to what extent should I give up mine?

I would give up a lot if I could insure my children's and grandchildren's happiness. To others though, not so much.

I guess I have answered that question. My giving is tight these days.

At my first Seder, at the Zaslow's, our Rabbi and Rebbetzin, we were all asked how we wanted to be better, what changes we wanted for ourselves. My response was, "To have a more generous spirit." I believe in the years since then, almost ten, I have achieved much of what I sought.

It does not seem the sort of thing one can only will. The key is in paying attention to others, watching, listening, hearing, and for sure, willing.

I love going to Rainey's, our corner market.

The first thing I like is getting out of the car and hearing country music that blares out to the parking lot from the store. Going in there in my worn out jeans, old shirt, no makeup, let alone a bra. In that moment, I have become them. People I had never known.

One old man is always there. No teeth, shuffling, white beard. The clerks always make sure he is okay. A woman, also with no teeth, and a child denied an extra candy bar, but with a husband checking out a twelve pack of beer.

The clerk in the hardware section saying, "Wow, you need more hoses?" Remembered us but I not her. We had bought hoses last week.

They all love Dave. They are getting reacquainted with me now that I am always with him. They know I am the one in charge.

Before now, I was able to call the store if he checked out the same item twice, which happened frequently. He'd pay in the back of the store, the hardware section, then again in front at the groceries and not notice he'd paid twice.

"It is fine, no problem, we'll fix it." They took such good care of him. Shopped with him if necessary. Simple people? Not so simple, I am the simple one with my hierarchal view of what constitutes degrees of complexity – perhaps I overvalue education…not education, educated people. Ironic if one considers who gets the world in such a fix.

Last Sunday, we had a huge cart full because we never go to a regular market anymore. A smiling country man behind us with one bottle of Australian beer. Was no never mind to him that he had to wait.

Our check-out had already started, so nothing to do. The sweet guy even went back and checked on the price of Saran Wrap for us.

Our alfalfa supplier, a mile away, was born here. Born in Sam's Valley. Dale Shultz, in his seventies by now.

Every year he brings in the hay. Each year the months between deliveries go faster for us both. I always say the same thing, "Weren't you just here?" And he always says with his charming grin, "Seems like it."

Yeah, we are them. We will miss this. If we go. If we ever have to go.

January 16, 2006

I learned just today that cats have no clavicle so can squeeze through any hole no wider than their head. I want to be a cat. Escape through a tiny opening. I am (again) starting to be nervous, a little afraid.

Today, putting the mailing labels on the real estate brochures, he could not keep it together. He stopped and stared at his work; he hoped to find the clue that would help him move on.

I don't think I can leave him to another place, with another to care for him, until he does not know much of anything.

My children want to save me so I can enjoy more of my life now. They want me to get help, possibly even move him now.

I wonder what decision I will make. I do not now know.

On my death bed, which choice would I regret?

Chapter 8

January 17, 2006

I worked on the newsletter all day. It's looking good, lots of input from members. The *New Song Voice* of Havurah Shir Hadash, my Jewish Renewal community. A passion of mine. The newsletter and the community.

Interrupted from time to time to take care of the business of our lives: Dave didn't know where to put a hanger. No special hanger, just one that belongs in a closet. Whether his or mine might have been the problem.

I got the bird food out late and wonder what they eat when I don't provide for them. How long could Dave find food for himself if I were not here to feed him? He would finish off the ice cream, move on to the peanut butter and jam. He might remember the soup in the cupboard and perhaps the food in the freezer though whether he would know what to do with either I'm not sure.

For a moment I considered not feeding the sheep and llamas...so rainy and cold. Now, once a day to go feed does not seem like much when I remember how much more strenuous it used to be.

Even as recently as two years ago, I would have been going out to the barns to check the ewes for possible birthing. Every four hours, night and day. Those four in the morning checks were a killer. Especially if a birth was imminent—no going back to bed. One night I got hypothermia and had to stand in the warm shower for a long time.

In the early days, I slept in the barn during lambing. Pretty wonderful. One night I remember especially. There were already five or six babies in the lambing barn. To them I was a familiar mom. They all snuggled up against me on my sleeping bag. That's a little bit of heaven. The smell of a baby lamb is one of the things I would like to experience again—all soft and milky and animally.

Oh yes, I will miss this. *If we go.*

January 18, 2006

The upside of the dogs getting old is Cindy, now fifteen or so, is deaf, and Meggi, only a bit younger, is getting there. They can't hear the coyotes howling at night, no longer wake me with a shriek-bark. Which was worse than annoying, they are heart stopping.

Now, at only 6:04 in the evening they are cackling up a storm, the coyotes. Five of them came in this morning to get the last two roosters. They missed.

I heard the roosters' alarm. There is no mistaking it. Ran out to look. The dogs had heard it also, or felt my alarm. Loping off across the pasture, dandy as you please were two young ones, then a third, then two more. I had never seen more than three together, older pups. I am guessing these were adolescent litter mates. Seems an odd time of year for pups, but if they are like dogs, season does not play a part in their cycles. Still, it seems a bit late for the litter to still be together, but with this many squirrels around, they may have found their spot.

In the end, this is what made us quit breeding the ewes. We lost so many lambs to them. High fencing, daily filling holes beneath the fences, dogs, llamas, did no good.

At one point early on when we realized the coyotes were coming in, Dave bought a gun, a *twenty-two* I think. He knew about guns from his stint in Korea. Well, I wasn't too keen on his trying to shoot the wily fellows, but I needn't have worried: he purposely shot so high above them, I was afraid he might hit a bird!

Since I would not kill them, there was nothing to do but give up to them their occasional prey, my little lambs. They do not come after the adults. The rams weigh 175 to 250 pounds; coyotes do not have the jaws of wolves.

Those who were here
Before our encroachment
Were welcomed by us.
How little did we know that it was
They who allowed us?

They would take their due
From time to time.
The Coyote, the Vulture,
The Crow, the Fly, the Wasp,
And the Maggot.

I do not want ever to forget this gut wrencher (though maybe I should). Years ago, I called animal control to see what could be done about the coyotes killing our lambs. This was probably around 1987. We had been here raising sheep for three years. All of a sudden losing lambs, eight. Believe me, it is monstrous, the little dead body being dragged off. Or it is left with a hole in its throat; even if momentarily saved, the poor thing cannot eat or drink and succumbs to infection.

But I did not hate them, the coyotes. They were doing their thing. And they are so beautiful. They trot across the field with such command. When they are fleeing our yelling, they go with a lope that reminds me of horses on a carousel. They jump the fences as easily as the deer. When they hunt the ground creatures, they are as funny as kittens with a mouse.

So this old trapper comes in, name of Obie, old scratchy faced fellow. Belongs to the county program.

He has a caged raccoon in the back of his truck. I look at her and say, "Oh, how cute she is." He says, "No Missy, she is not cute, she is mean."

Oh, oh, we are in trouble now.

The thing he will do, says he, is put loop traps along the fence holes on our and our neighbor's properties, the ones leading to the woods. We will get permission. He will post signs so the farmers will watch that their dogs and cats don't caught, or if caught, there is a release mechanism.

If I had known what was coming, I never would have agreed. The county trappers are supposed to come back every day to check the traps and shoot the caught coyotes. He did not come back for five days. Five caught coyotes. Caught, died there, rotting and fly blown.

Ah, what regret overtook me. Who are these people who have so little regard for a live being they have no care for its suffering? When the coyotes returned years later, we had no choice but to let them be.

Good thing happening now. That fun silly movie *Trading Places* is on. Dave named both Eddie Murphy and Don Ameche. And we both, after a moment, got Ralph Bellamy. Any time he can recall is a burst for me.

January 20, 2006

I am thinking maybe the reason I write so much about animals, and fallen trees here and in my poetry, is that being human can be the pits.

I am weary of being a character in someone else's life. I am tired of cats yowling, dogs in my way tripping me, demanding, let me in, let me out, feed me, pet me. And this husband who needs constant attention.

This is my life. It is a conundrum; I want fewer responsibilities but adore the creatures I am responsible for. I would like to be dramatic and say, *THIS IS MY LIFE*, but in fact, it is in small letters, no different from any others.

Tonight was horrible. As usual, I am so tired. Kathy and Simone were coming for Shabbat dinner. Cannot call and say, no, please no, do not come.

They arrived, wired, back from Simone's school day in town. Kathy brought dinner fixings and made it. But nothing will do other than Simone being the center of attention as always.

At the end of dinner, Simone having been encouraged by Kathy to play on her own had set up a little village. Dave, unaware, stepped on it and destroyed her creation. Understandably, she had a hissy fit.

For me the screaming and its cause were too much. I appealed to Kathy: "I cannot take this, you have to go."

Simone kept screaming that she wanted her ice cream.

I took the ice cream out to the car... and her shoes. Gathering up, leaving...out at the car Kathy wanted none of it. She was angry. I tried to explain...I was freaked that Dave destroyed her project, how difficult the last few days had been.

What she said was, "Why blame it on her, she is only four years old?"

Yes, and I am sixty-two.

On page 58 of *The Little Prince*, there is his conversation with the snake:

"But I am more powerful than the finger of a king," said the snake.

The little prince smiled.

"You are not very powerful. You haven't even any feet. You cannot even travel…"

"I can carry you farther than any ship could take you," said the snake.

The silver coil of the snake around my ankle.

That is where I want to go, farther than any ship could take me. Not to Death, to Peace.

Chapter 9

JANUARY 22, 2006

Dave responds to just about anything with his mantra: *Well, that's Mother Nature.*

He says it to Peter, our UPS driver, Bruce, our mechanic, Dale, our hay provider, the clerks at Rainey's. I am guessing it is his way of being present, in the conversation.

Sometimes it is about *Mother Nature.* Today he came up with a different one. He loves Beth, my best friend. And no wonder, she is so sweet with him, absolutely never condescending (as I frequently am). She treats him as an equal player. She has helped my talking to him work better, e.g. "Refer to objects by color rather than name: Pass the blue things next to your elbow."

When I play back my voice mail, he hears her voice, and always asks, "Did you get the message from Beth?" Never mind that, *hello,* I am the one retrieving it. (See what I mean about condescension?)

Many times, as I prepare to call her back, he says, "Tell Beth I said 'Hi'."

She and I had one of our good, long, conversations last night. Over and over this morning, this afternoon, Dave asked, "How is Beth, how is she doing?"

Then asked, "How old is her daughter?" I gave the answers: Claudia is Kathy's age, forty-four. She is the one with the four children who lives in Reno. Sarah is a few years older and lives in

San Francisco (didn't get into dear Katie who is in a special space Beth barely can penetrate.)

He : Well, all on the West coast. Then he invoked what I know will be a new mantra: "Well, that's *modern times.*"

He has something in his head, not sure if it is about families separated, or families separated but still near. There is so much going on he can no longer articulate.

And losing words: this afternoon he asked if he should go up and get the "film." He meant mail. Though many times I had told him today was Sunday, no mail. We do, however, watch a lot of film and take a lot of videos.

When his parents visited years ago, it is clear to me now his mother was in a pretty far advanced stage of Alzheimer's, more than Dave is now. Every time the word *"well"* came in the conversation, she would say "That's a deep subject" and chuckle. We all had to chuckle too. I would have preferred to shake her and say, *"Get a grip."*

And the forever wanting to know where her pocketbook was. (Snob that I am, even offended by the word pocketbook...it's a purse!) Over and over, *Mom, it is right next to you.*

I love the Pennsylvania Dutch saying: *too soon old, too late smart.*

That woman was the reason for Dave's sweetness and generosity. His father, an autocratic egotist. But sharp, smart, funny. My step-father to a tee. But also, a sadist just under the skin. This jerk told a story at our dinner table about a scene he had witnessed when he was a boy: about cannibalistic pigs. I wish I didn't remember it.

I knew nothing about dementia. I saw her, Dave's Mom (re-named from Peggy to Pansy), as a downtrodden woman, not one demented. We went to Ashland to cruise the shops, and to have lunch at my sister and brother-in-law's restaurant (truly the best hamburgers in town, my sister the dynamite cook.) Dave's Mom didn't know what to order, "I said, it is up there, up on the menu."

She was clueless. I misinterpreted it as complete subservience to her husband who said, "She likes me to do it for her."

This woman was daft. I did not see it. My lenses were clouded.

Oh my love, my darling...

I am not objecting to your going to bed in the clothes you have worn for three days, day and night.

You are a clean, clean man, so what is the big deal, why impose my stuff? What's the dif'? Just eat the food and take the pills, and give me a kiss...

January 23, 2006

Related by Kathy this morning:
Simone: "I love going to Grandma's ."
Kathy: "Yeah ."
Simone: "No, I *really* love going to Grandma's, *as big as a heart.*"

Tonight's theme is accompanied by Joe Cocker's *You are so beautiful to me.*

I am beginning to accept my old face. I think of the old faces I know and love. Why not my own?

Today is Linda Lewis' 63rd birthday. We were best friends in junior high, mid-fifties. One night at a party of dancing and delighting in each other, we, side by side, looked in the mirror to determine who was the most beautiful that night. Each of us thought we had won the contest.

Dave's face is only a little old although thirteen years my senior. If he were standing with us, Linda and me, I would have seen such a boy, a lot like Donny, my boyfriend then. It could have been Dave, a charming, cute, sexy scamp, joking to deflect the emotion.

(Oh, those days for me and mine. No questioning, no drink, no drugs. Parents who knew they were training us to join society so provided the opportunities for us.)

Back to faces. Tonight watching a sweet and funny British comedy, *As Time Goes By,* then whoops, here it is again: Judy Dench. What a beautiful face! *Nu*, I am not that beautiful? So what?

And Beth, and another friend Jonnie—it is in their eyes, in their smile, and indeed in the crinkly wrinkles that speak of years of being fully engaged in life.

I have the eyes, the smile, the wrinkles. I have a granddaughter for whom being with me is as *"big as a heart."*

And *this* woman, not beautiful in the usual sense, but what a presence, a gift. May Sarton left an impressive legacy of over fifty books, including novels, poetry, memoirs and journals. Her appeal lay in her ability to: *"sacramentalize the ordinary"* by probing everyday subjects such as flowers, gardens, animals, changing sunlight and personal relationships in order to find deeper, universal truths.

I want to do that, hope to do that with this Diary. Kathy just brought four of her journals back from the library for me so I can try to figure out why I like her writing so much.

First, though, I am impelled to finish the Jonathan Kellerman, 2/3 through, cannot let a mystery go. (Ah, and the mystery of Dave, of our lives – will I solve that one?)

Then will gobble up the Journals as I do with caviar and champagne. The caviar on buttered toast with chopped onions on the side.

Oh, will that ever happen again? Will I ever see Paris again?

Oh, poor me............. Well there are always the bluebirds... Hah!

Chapter 10

JANUARY 24, 2006

I am getting sick of myself.

It is only five-thirty, we have just had peanuts while watching our early cop shows.

I left him with the British comedy saying I would be back in a few minutes; I need to write. No sooner do I sit down than I hear him rummaging around. Go out to check. He has this huge bowl of ice cream.

"We haven't had dinner yet, we usually eat around six. Shall I put something different on the TV? Shall I make dinner now?"

"No, I'm fine...what do you want me to do? Do you want me to put it back?"

He should not eat so much sugar. His brother has diabetes. Alzheimer's is associated with high insulin levels.

Am I upset because:

1. He is doing what he should not be
2. Or because I am in here, not out there, doing my duty, watching that he doesn't harm himself
3. Or because, it just *isn't right* to eat ice cream before dinner?

This urge to keep imposing my *dos* and *don'ts* is becoming a very irritating habit—irritating for both of us.

Last night when we went to bed he was, again, fully clothed. I asked him to take off his sweater and shirt at least. He said, "No, it keeps me warm."

I was with him in bed, our usual before sleep cuddle, and did not want the clothes between skin and skin. Said, "Okay, I'll just get another man." (Is that horrible or what?)

"Do you want another man?"

"No, I just want you to take your clothes off!"

But by then, when he tried to oblige, I was so sorry for what I might have put in his psyche, I said, "No, it's fine, we can cuddle like this."

And now, back to earlier this night: he has gone to bed with no dinner.

I answered a call from my sister, who also needs me right now, to talk, to commiserate, and to join experiences.

So, when I am not there with him watching TV, he apparently cannot be there either.

The tight grasp of guilt that I am not doing my job.
I did say "for better or for worse" (Maybe… it seems standard).
I have no illusions that this is the "worse."
The worst is yet to come, I have no doubt.

Yesterday he backed the truck into the Buick, smashed the side.

Bruce, our mechanic, had come to see about the clanking noise of the truck. And why the Buick was stuck, right there in the road. Just stopped. Broken axle. He pushed it over to the side. $150 to fix it. I said, "Okay, it will give Dave a vehicle to go up and down the road, and to Rainey's."

Truck: maybe a broken crank shaft (I must be the only person in the world who does not know what a crankshaft is; explanations do not help). Dead duck if it's the crankshaft. Ah! It's out of gas. Crank shaft (whatever that is) is not the problem.

So, Dave, after Bruce put in some gas, maneuvered the truck to go get the paper. And smashed plumb into the Buick, the dead duck without an axle.

I so love these slow motion scenes. You just know it is going to happen. All you can do is watch. This whole scene played in my mind as though from afar. *Laurel and Hardy* crossed my mind. Or a surreal dream sequence both ridiculous and sublime. And if a good story, a laugh.

January 25, 2006

Feeling a little fractured. When we lived in California I was doing art, Dave was playing his horn. We had conversations about what motivated us, where the exhilaration came from.

He could not imagine playing without an audience. That makes sense for a musician, especially a trumpet player whose soul moves from his emotions to his brain to his lungs and then through the horn. This is how he plays.

For me, the process was the whole thing. The end product? Usually it was there ahead of me. I just needed to find out what it was: *what color, shape was meant to be in this spot?*

It was nice having other people see it, especially if they liked it. But the hours in my little art room, making the stuff, running down in the morning to look at it again. That was the real deal—that's what charged my batteries.

Apparently, Boswell said there is no point in writing except for money. Can't imagine where I read that just the other day. Anyway, he was full of BS if he meant it, which I seriously doubt, surely an irony.

I can just see it:

"Oh Mr. Boswell, how beautifully you write!

And pray tell, what inspires you? How do you sit down each long day with pen and ink to put all those words together? Truly, what inspires you?"

"Money, madam, money."

Hah! Mr. Boswell, walk in my shoes. Writing is my salvation...Art.
Both imagination and reality ground me.

Imagining I can just see a support group:

Well, Michelle, we have all gone through this: You are very sad you are losing your man.

"You feel guilty when you are frustrated with him."

"You miss your other life, not just your life together, but that you cannot have the part of your life that was yours apart from him—your friends and activities."

"You think you do not know very well how to care for him. What you think is best is not always what he wants, let alone agrees to. When you help him put on his sweater, he says, 'I can do it myself.' He does not remember that three weeks ago he tried to put it on as though it were pants, over his legs."

"And you want to say, *screw you, do it yourself*. But you don't because you begin to understand what it must be like."

And everyone will say, "It is only natural, normal, we all go through this."

And you know what:

Go through it yourselves, because if I were here, I would take each one of you home with me in my heart and cry for you. I would take on your tears too.

But I do not need any more dependents.

Chapter 11

༄

Old Man
Old man, you are gone from me
Your teeth leave your head, but you do not know
You look at your food as though it is a chess move
But then, you look up and ask,
"Hey Babe, how are you today?"
Gone. or temporarily absent?
Old man.

༄

JANUARY 29, 2006

He is a bit confused this morning, although he made his usual entrance into my office with a greeting and a funny. We watched a bit of CBS Morning (Jimmy Carter is amazing at 88.)

Then he said he sensed a shower coming. I said, "Yes, a good idea."

He: "Where should I take it? In the house? Back there?"

A bit later, I went in to make our bed and was startled by him coming out of my bathroom with nail clippers and the powder container of cornstarch he uses for talc. He asked me if I wanted the nail clippers as he had a pair. Apparently he had taken them from my drawer, asked where he should put the talc: "In the kitchen?"

I guess because he knows it comes from there, he forgets it belongs in the bathroom. Later I realize he has been in my bathroom to dry his hair, he forgot I replaced his broken hair dryer a couple of weeks ago.

I kept reminding him to shave. He has always been fastidious (and a little vain), endearing really.

After he dressed, (again with the dressing, such a test for me,) wearing for some reason his fancy loafers, I gave him a sweater to put on, as he is often cold. "Where should I put it?" he asks. Although last week he was annoyed with me for helping him dress, I did this time anyway after he tried to put his shirt over his legs. Apparently he welcomes my help sometimes.

This slope is a gentle one with flat spots along the way, meadows even.

I am charmingly kind and patient and relaxed after a good yesterday.

Next, he goes out to feed the chickens, walking through mud. Tracking it back through the house. He shuffles now rather than walks, so really digs in the dirt. A white Berber carpet, very receptive to chunks of mud. What could we possibly have been thinking, we live on a farm! At that point, I become a little impatient —why won't he grasp what needs to be done and take off his shoes?

He is settled in now, working on the mailings, his favorite thing.

His fastidiousness reminds me of our family joke about his not wanting to get wet.

He and Kathy and I were on our boat, a beautiful nice tight Santana. We were on a reach, the fastest tack, from the harbor to the Malibu promontory. It was very windy and choppy. A beautiful day. Moving along, on the track. There's this groove you and the boat take, there is no missing it, just you and the wind, the digging in of the keel, the holding of the main and the jib. This boat! You are part of it!

We were flying! Kathy and I, laughing and laughing and loving it. Dave, not so much. Sprays up over the bow, nothing to it, not washes. No Titanic here. And the sun was out. But Davey doesn't like to get wet. Grumpy for the rest of the trip.

Once, I threw a glass of water at an obnoxious man. Dave has been afraid one day I will do that to him.

Never.

January 30, 2006

I had forgotten how much fun creative energy can be. It is around me right now, seeing some of the evolution of a friend's book, the decisions, and the changes. And, the possibility I may be writing something. Well, of course I am writing something. But the possibility someone will read and enjoy it, take it to heart.

And! Kathy searching for a new career, one she will suck into her bones for her own energy and so be able to give back.

Something about Social Enterprises. Helping non-profits to create income producing businesses that will fund the socially important activity, and also train and enable others to learn a… whatever: skill, craft, awareness of social obligations.

Or, something she is even more excited about: focused communities with specific goals, enlarging their support system themselves; not fund raising but self supporting through their own enterprise. She has read about many of these around the world.

Her excitement excites and empowers me. I lost that somewhere in the last couple of years. Maybe it was deciding having lambs was too much, and in losing that close tie with creation I lost some of my own creativity and the energy that comes from that source.

Of course, that was the energy of the lambs and the ewes, not mine. I partook, and of course, did all the work to make it happen, let's not be too modest here.

It really was the coyotes cutting the babies down, that finally got to me, not Dave's condition that rendered him unable to be as much involved with the animal husbandry. It was not my own diminishing abilities, my aging that forced the decision. Well, and no wonder, I was ever alert, always afraid for them. Not to mention going to the barns every four hours to check on the birthings.

But very little in my life has been more wonderful. An emerging lamb, the dropping lamb, a pile of sweet smelling wet, slippery skin, shaking head, tiny bleats. The mom up on her feet clucking, licking, loving with all her heart. There is nothing in her life right now but that baby. Later she will take some food and water, but not now. Her job, her life's job, is to get that baby on its feet and suckling.

Time later for the rest of her life.

The image of the lion and the lamb is not for nothing. Nothing more vulnerable than a lamb.

Ah, and you may say, but what about a human child?

Well, I will tell you. When the coyotes come after the lambs, the ewes are afraid also. And run. They do miss their lamb, but they consider their own life more precious. Of course, they think none of this. They are the prey and the predator is coming.

Though I have heard it happens, I imagine it is a rare human mother who runs ahead of her child from danger. A hen does not. That I have seen many times. Though I could be wrong. And hope I am.

My own mother ran ahead of my chaser. Well, she was not seeing the danger and so not running herself really. Maybe, I do not know.

I really hate being sidetracked to this, I wish I could be done with it once and for all.

What I do know is I have such a good man here. I am strong. I am well. I am woman. I chose right the second time!

So the irony. No, of course not, life has no ironies for me...the ironies are my own perception.

I do not believe in destiny, karma, God looking over me. What is, is. Duh (as the kids say, and I love it, use it all the time.)

He has a disease. In no time there will be a cure. Not for him.

Yesterday, he came with me out to the barn to feed. He could not follow the direction, just kept looking to me. As though he could see in my eyes where to put the feed.

And why not, his life is in my eyes now. And my heart.

And I work to make it good, but do not succeed as well as I would like. The reconditioned trumpet lies idle in the closet, my forgetting to encourage him. The old broken tape deck not replaced so he doesn't hear himself anymore. That beautiful sound.

January 31, 2006

Can't seem to find the source for "Love is the question, not the answer."

If I made that up, I would be excited, but like all my stuff, it'd been said before, though, maybe in a different order.

This old dog, my collie Meggi, is in here with me. Her nails clack on the floor and make me crazy. I hate the sound. She, now in her dotage, wants only me.

I do love her, dread the day of putting her down; I hope I awake one morning and she is gone. Just like that.

So, what does love require? How nice if we knew the rules.

I put her out of the room; after all, she is *just* a dog.

Barbara Kingsolver has a wonderful book (among many), *Prodigal Summer*.

Her woman lives in a cabin. I will take that solitary life in nature. But not really. It is only a metaphor for escaping the pain of loving.

Had a long talk today with a good friend. She is suffering the pain of loving. Her child has become not herself, or the way she was.

Loving a child is the ultimate joy, the ultimate vulnerability. My scariest times have always been fear for them.

Pacing and pacing waiting to know that Jennifer, my precious younger daughter, and Ari were safe at his birth. The doctor had said, "You will see your grandson in an hour." It seemed, and was, longer.

And then, the face of Jennifer, reflecting the amazement of a new life, absorbing the face of her beautiful new child. "Hey little one let's see what you look like." There is no describing it, though I do have the video, memories no longer needed, God forbid that would happen.

I remember clearly the day I knew this beautiful, strong, intelligent woman was alive. My OB-Gyn asked if I wanted more children. I smiled, "Yes, there is one more waiting to be born." Neither of us knew at that time I was a few weeks pregnant.

Why did I not have Dave with me for Ari's birth? Looking back it seems peculiar. We have had relatives come before to farm sit. I think I sometimes I want my children for myself only. The strongest bond. It was still the early stages of his disease and he was able to handle taking care of things himself, I thought.

But when I called one day, he said one of the ewes had died. And then the oddest explanation: "I didn't call the vet earlier because I thought she would be dead by now." He did call the vet a few days later when she did not die as he expected.

I never think of the births of my grandchildren without this one. Kathy, during Simone's birth, pouring out blood. If her life was seeping out, as it seemed it was, I would have made a pact with the Devil to save her. The most frightening day of my life.

I didn't need to have make that pact. A first rate doctor assured that a few years later I would be hearing, "Let's play, Grandma, come on Grams, let's get started!"

And another occasion of mother angst, my heart breaking at a lunch with Patrick. Mothers' Day in Chicago when we went to the aquarium.

He told me he had not been able to enjoy his graduate work for worrying about finding a teaching/research position at a university. By that day, he had already been hired, but his sadness in giving up so much to the worrying was the pain for me.

On balance, he committed to not being a star in the show, as he told me then, though not in those words, but rather to be a father to his sons, a husband to his wife.

Turned out, he *is* a star in the show. He has brought millions in grants for Evolutionary Biology at University of Oregon.

Hey, what goes around. Maybe there is something out there after all. The good people win? In spite of my feeling I should do more for Dave, perhaps because he is one of the good people, he does have me and it is enough.

Chapter 12

FEBRUARY 2, 2006

I was going to take a few days break from writing, but my head keeps talking and talking.

As part of the break, we were going to watch some movies, not just our usual TV re-runs of old favorites. So, tonight *Wings of Desire*.

Oh my, that is really something, an angel falls in love with a circus performer. But I didn't last long. As soon as I heard, read actually, the spoken words are in German:

"*I know so little, maybe I'm too curious. I often think wrongly. Because I think as though I were talking to someone else.*"

Well, of course I bolted out of the living room to come to the office in order to write and tell all those who might someday read this, *Hey, that is me: I am always talking to you! All day long, I am writing in my head.*

Too funny, crazy people are *just us* only more so.

Dave has gone to a spot that seems so free. Nothing to worry about, responsibilities over. A child again. With a strong mommy to take care of him.

Sometimes I would like to go there, but only if it did not hurt.

And it must. He grabs at words. I do also, we all do. His grabbing is more painful, because in a few seconds, he forgets what he has been grabbing for.

I remember another damaged man and our conversation, Ron, from A-Z Auto Wrecking, maybe it is Auto Saving, I forget. Our connection is what I want to talk about.

We donated the Taurus Beth gave us to the Kidney Foundation. Ron was their guy, the man who took the cars, and did something with them. He arrives, sets up his big rig and attaches all sorts of stuff to the car to get it ready to tow.

Oh, did I mention, it is night. Dark night. He apologizes. As though one needs to apologize for the night. Not your job, man.

So we are tossing small talk as he does his stuff. Then the meat for all of us, Dave included. We really talk, somehow about contributing. The Korean War comes into it (Dave's service.)

Ron is a little guy and clearly physically askew. So my question, "Were you hurt in the war?"

Turns out, no, he was severely injured in an accident, not expected to walk, let alone work. A great story about survival, about not giving up.

And so he talks about *giving*, about caring for and about people. About having come back determined to show he is grateful for his life by sharing it, giving to others.

We three have a connection, we are all generous people—I work at it, for Dave it comes naturally.

Because I liked him and his attitude, I called him the other day, to tell him I wanted to give him the Buick. And by the by (wish it were not so) our truck was stuck in the mud, would he pull it out on the way in? Not a trade, the Buick is his.

He said, "I would do anything for you, you are such a sweetheart."

People think that about me. It is true a lot of the time, but not always. I can do things I hate when others do them: today I killed a black widow because I was too lazy to take her out to the creek and let her go. She was asleep, hibernating, would not have noticed. I noticed. And regretted.

I want to be awake the moment before I die.

FEBRUARY 4, 2006

Oh, laws, blah, blah, blah. Whoever heard of someone being bored by her own diary? Well, that is some joke I haven't read it yet. Maybe it is fascinating.

Oh laws is something Kathy and I say. Now, she more than I. I started it. Not sure where I got it. It is that big sigh with words attached. Probably comes from *oh Lordy me,* or *Lawdy Lawdy, Miss Claudy*, the Lloyd Price song.

Big relief: Jennifer is shet of her depression. Talked to her last night on her cell; she was driving to the city to meet friends for drinks and dinner.

Oh, nothing to it. Wow, just drive into NY for the evening. Last week she went in to see the new *Sweeney Todd*. Oh, we did laugh, neither of us have a clue what it is about. The next day she called Andrew, who studied Sondheim at U.C. Santa Cruz, to get his take.

I am so relieved they are still friends even through the impending divorce. Their shared custody of the boys is the shared custody of love, their past, and the love each will always have for their children.

I called Patrick Thursday night to tell him of my excitement about the frogs. I always e-mail him when the frogs start, but this was special. Had to call instead.

I walked out to feed in the afternoon, and just sensed *frogs"*— no sound, no calendar, just farm sense.

Oh, yes! after dark, the music of them. The first day of the frogs.

I called Dave to the door: *listen*. He: *crickets*. No, it's the frogs come back.

My call of excitement to Patrick was not that the frogs are back (though in the drought a few years ago, it was a concern), but that I sensed their starting their magic. I explained there was something about the air, the slow wind, the roar of the creek. I just knew it. And he *knew,* no explanation necessary.

He said, yes, there were the days, the air, when I knew it was the day to go out to the ponds. He studied frogs when he was at Reed.

I am the most fortunate of women. I am loved by and connected to my children.

FEBRUARY 5, 2006

Kindness. *Kindness of strangers*, but more particularly, the kindness of those of our hearts.

We just watched an episode of *Crossing Jordan*. Had its due share of malevolence, but more particularly, lack of trust, hardening of heart, the craziness of launching to the goal, mowing over those in your path—incomprehensible to me. Or maybe it was about something else entirely.

I get such a tremendous kick out of myself, as said in an earlier entry. The trying to be viewer, recorder, the philosopher (not too bad at that).

I stand back, and above, all the time, as though directing my own movie. Then the impersonal eye blinks, and I jump in and star, feeling it all.

Being with Simone today, working with her on a project, I scooped her into my memory... and knew I was doing it, *I am here now seeing this, this perfect arch of her neck as she leans down to retrieve the sticker. This soft cheek, the cut of her hair.*

I am writing my memories as I experience them. Trippy. Am I at last getting the writer's eye? And if I am, is it a distraction from the experience?

Oh isn't this great fun, being human, having a human brain.

Read an interview with the Dali Lama today. He acknowledges and accepts secular values as natural. A religious leader of such humanness and kindness.

Also read yesterday, a fascinating article, scientific, about why we are hard wired to believe in non-corporeal beings (gods, ghosts, angels, etc.).

And, soul-less physical beings, golems, Mary Wollstonecraft's Frankenstein.

I must be differently wired. Don't believe a word of any of it.

I believe in love, that kestrels do poop from the branch before they fly, that cats and dogs and sheep will manipulate you to be fed, that the happiness of children is more valuable than diamonds, and that the soft smell of the neck of the man in your bed makes life grand.

Chapter 13

FEBRUARY 6, 2006

My job now is to use common sense. Wanting to let Dave be as free as he had been used to being is not always in the best interest of either of us. Recalling his backing into the Buick made me realize this.

Another instance: miring the truck in the mud the other day, not just taking the off-road track to avoid the pot holes, but plowing a new track even further into the pasture.

It was pretty funny actually when all was resolved. I had seen only the right wheel, buried half up the hubcap. Turns out, the left wheel was buried to the tire top!

So what I am now accepting is his driving judgment is impaired. So, no more driving except up and down the driveway for the paper in the morning and the mail in the afternoon. Trash up on Thursday mornings. That way, I can conceal from him he is not allowed to drive. Lucky thing we have a third-of-a-mile driveway, it feels like going somewhere.

He was actually relieved the other day when I bopped up to Rainey's on my own. Out of cigarettes at 7:30 in the morning, but if I'm there, hey, a weeks worth of groceries too.

Initially he wanted to come: "It is what I should do, go with you."

He is my protector, has always seen himself as that. But happy not to have to change out of his slippers. Now, more and more, letting me take care of him.

Parents as protectors, each of us who love, protecting the one we love.

That crazy scene at the pool in Redondo Beach. We were on our honeymoon, with all the kids, naturally.

This macho man tossed Patrick into the pool. A big man picking on this skinny little ten-year-old boy. Dave and I were ready to kill. Patrick in the pool, waved and implored, "No stop, it's okay, I'm okay."

Who protects whom? And when? Sooner rather than later is the common sense way to go. But sometimes from the mouths of babes comes the reality, the sensible thing to do.

February 7, 2006

Dear Diary,

(May I call you dear? Or, may I call you, dear?) Sorry, too much time with silliness.

You, dear diary, who know me best, know how much ambivalence I live with these days.

To wit: right now, I want to pop up and check on Dave. I just gave him his dinner, realigned his plate when he lost it and went to get something else, put on one of the wonderful animal shows we both like.

Well, excuse me for a moment, I do need to do it, be right back. Compulsive, don't you know.

Ok, he's fine. When I tell him I am going to be working in the office, on my diary, he says: "Okay, take your time, enjoy yourself."

Now, why can't I just do that?

So tonight I was thinking, if we move to Ashland or Eugene, he could spend some time during the day in Trinity Respite or another facility (now I see I did say "facility," think that says what I am concerned about.)

Am I dumping him, abrogating my responsibility? Or saving some of my life? Certainly, I have as much a right to some of my life as he has to his. The difference is I have choices, he does not. What his rights are is entirely up to me. Can't say I care much for such a huge obligation.

And the other ambivalence: what to do if Kathy stays? What to do if Kathy leaves? She lives just a mile from us but feels isolated in the country.

Well, the leaving part is easy, I will follow. If she stays, will we stay here still or move to Ashland?

She is taking a huge leap into creating her own business. She may sell her home, take some of the money to rent a home and to support herself for six months until the business takes off.

I am so proud of her. I used to be a risk taker. Maybe a bit still.

This area or Eugene? Probably here to start. It is where our support systems are – family, friends, synagogue, community friends. Well, plenty of time, a bunch of relieving freedom to know there is time — time to plant broccoli, possibly even enough time for cosmos and tomatoes.

༄

Spikes of tall life gird your landscape
Yellow, rose, and violet set above your mounds
My farm...
Beasts roam
Birds flit
Geese honk in their vees
Poppies bloom.

> *Still, the Beast roars:*
> *"You cannot have it all,*
> *You have had enough;*
> *I will take it back,*
> *Why do you deserve more?"*

☙

And months more to live for the old sheep. That will be agony, to kill them because of my needing to move on, when I was the one who brought them to life.

Especially Black Magic, Fatty Patti, Tag Along, and Charlie. But why should I say that? How is it their lives are more valuable than Old One, Brenda's Boy, Hershey Jr.? I do not want this power.

I must decide if it is beyond repair, my agony. If it is, I will see them out on their own terms, when they decide to die.

Or maybe that is my way of staying here. Instead perhaps find a little place with a couple of acres so to bring them with us.

Still, they don't care the reason, dead is dead.

God must be aghast about what his children are doing. That too few of us think of these things, about *all* living creatures and how we are entwined.

Yes, I do count myself on the good side. Not ego, humility. The 'whole' is too much for me.

February 8, 2006

I wonder if this conflictedness is becoming addictive, sort of like adrenaline soup.

Just now, I sat down to write, to start by saying "I am so sick of TV that even the company of strangers would be better."

But first went in to check on Dave. He was standing at the window. I went to look with him, he showed me the pink striped sky. And my eye caught through the window a sight I love, the long driveway, the perfect fence line he put up. One third mile all on his own.

It was so easy then. All we did here. He built two barns by himself. Well, he allowed a little help from me on the second.

Just writing this makes me sad. Not many would be able physically to put up a barn alone at seventy-six. But someone that age without Alzheimer's would be able to see the missing board on a fence and replace it. He is physically strong enough; it is the *pattern* he cannot grasp.

Now, back to the conflictedness, no segue intended, there is one somewhere in the under run, the "under toad," as John Irving would say. Kathy and I were talking about it this morning. I had forgotten to add that if I move to Ashland, my employer in the marketing work I do, will suck me in. She has continually implored me to return as her assistant…just a little bit to start.

As well she might, I was good.

If Dave had some daytime place to go once in a while, I would be tempted.

What temptations do I want to realize? Way too many: I want it all, (but willing to trade. If the price is right. I now, unlike when I was 23, count the costs).

I love working, doing something. How much reading can a person do before she comes out and joins life?

I weeded a bit late this afternoon, pulling the grass from the emerging tiny bulb shoots.

Takes such finesse, gently uptaking the grass roots, shaking them a bit underground so as not to undermine the desired ones.

FEBRUARY 9, 2006

April is the cruelest month, breeding Lilacs out of the dead land, mixing Memory and desire, stirring / Dull roots with spring rain.

I know perfectly well these lines of Eliot's have nothing whatever to do with gardening.

But I will bet you dollars to donuts I am not the only gardener today who takes them over for herself, with her own meaning. A perfect beginning of a spring day. The air just soft, the sun just low, warm only, still, first shorts and tee shirt of the year. Ah, it is rather a day like this in February that is the cruelest.

Never have I had nothing to do in the garden, but rarely more nothing than today. Well, just a bit. Disengaging the young shoots from the grass and other weeds is the most nurturing but tiresome of jobs. Especially because the soil is wet, frozen in places.

Maybe we gardeners suppose we are working with plants, landscapes, home ambiance. Not to mention the dirt. The dirt is the best part. Good dirt. Enriched, loose, feeder dirt. The ground. Yes, we are doing that. And, also spacing out beyond whatever ails us. Every metaphor we could ask for is here.

And, by chance, but with favorable odds, Dylan is now singing *Trying to Get to Heaven Before They Close the Door.*

"When you think you've lost everything, you find out you can lose a little more."

This is exactly what I am trying to avoid. I cannot decide if I wish it were out of my hands or not. But how funny. What a funny thing to say. I do what I do, I make this and that decision, I act as though it were in my hands. That is me. But if it is not, hey, maybe a relief. Sometimes I envy Dave, he has no decisions to make.

Chapter 14

FEBRUARY 10, 2006

I want to be sure I do not take out on Dave whatever I may not like about my life.

Or, the corollary, what I perceive he is doing that prevents my doing what I want with my life. I make choices, he forces nothing on me.

He is as he is now. There is no longer anything to rage against. And I am committed. Breaking vows with this man would be a stain on my soul. *In sickness and in health, from this day forward, 'til death do us part.*

We had a few rough times. The horrible time in Portland stands out as the worst. Jennifer graduated high school in June of 1984—we uprooted the next day and moved to Ashland. A few weeks later we took her to Portland to start her freshman year at Reed. It was very hard for both of us to be leaving our last child; we were emotionally fragile. All kids were in the car, Patrick already lived on campus, but we were on a night out, a little vacation.

Dave kept getting lost over the bridges and refused to listen to my suggestions. After a half hour, I just went ballistic. I raged at him for choosing what I knew was the wrong exit.

The next morning, without telling us, Dave bought a ticket back to Medford and just left! And on to Florida to be with his parents. His family. He was sick of mine.

Kathy and I drove home. Down the coast. A beautiful drive, stopped everywhere to look over the cliffs at the ocean. Wandered off the path to find special places.

Along the way, we passed a dead porcupine at the side of the road. We stopped the car to look at it. We had never seen a porcupine that close; Kathy took out a camera to take a picture, then stopped. We were both teary, mourning a little. Together, "Why would we want a picture of a dead porcupine?"

Once again, my life, a metaphor. We were both sad about this crazy acting man, this special man, jumping away from us because of my prickliness. He came back soon of course.

And, so, now here he is, twenty-two years later, still special but now a bit crazy for real.

February 11, 2006

A new strategy. A new way of being together. I will learn about Dave. Not insist he come to me.

Tonight we were watching some news. I said, "That is ridiculous."

He: "Yeah, Dickhead!"

Where he got that is a mystery, never used before. A great laugh for us both, after my: "What!!??"

(I don't cotton to profanity, for the most part, except funny works, and of course, I be the judge).

I went in later to check if what he was watching was okay with him: Winter Olympics. We have always so much loved the figure skating. The Ice Dancing was on, a beautiful long legged and lyrical couple, dressed in black.

He: "Finally, the Germans are not getting shot."

I bristled, "What do you mean? It was the Jews getting shot, not the Germans."

Then I scrunched down and looked at him: "Do you mean the Germans are not shooting anymore? That they are dancing instead?"

He nodded and nodded, "Yes, right, right."

I know that is what he meant.

I do this, and much else in my life, for love. But I bet the karma's dandy.

FEBRUARY 13, 2006

Dave's birthday. 76th.

Simone and I baked a cake in secret, chocolate with chocolate frosting. She put on all the candles. Asked how old he was. She was ready for the job of seventy-six candles.

Oh, my love, my heart, both of them.

She quickly grasped that we did not have 76 candles. Made instead a most perfect grouping of ten or so. Right in the middle. Ten pink candles on a dark chocolate cake.

Kathy came with a gift. He was surprised, kept forgetting it is his birthday. But: "Oh yes, I thought it was around now."

He was a little teary and appreciated the gesture, Kathy's gift of all the food goodies he loves. After they left, he said, "Well, that was quite a festivity, all the little kids running around, and all the big kids running around, having a good time." There was only Kathy and Simone.

Oh laws. What will become of us?

One of the positive (for me only) things is I am becoming more and more honest. I was about to say, *forced* into it. Not true. I am embracing it on my own. Always hated lies, covertness, and hidden agendas. Pretending.

How can I be true in my own life without knowing what is real around me? And that includes the *me* around *me*.

Today, a beautiful afternoon. *If things were different, I would go out on the deck, enjoy the sunset, and sit in a comfortable chair. Read a little, a crossword puzzle maybe.*

But would I really, alone? Is he my excuse for not "doing nothing whatever?" No, the truth is, I like doing "nothing whatever." But the list of things to do, and whom to become, is endless. So much easier, though not at all satisfying, is staying plopped in place. Could be the right thing to do, the default mode, which is always "suggested." But only by computers.

I am trying to juggle what I *should* be doing and what I *need* to do. Does everyone find balancing this difficult? Do they constantly judge themselves?

Chapter 15

FEBRUARY 15, 2006

I just had a long, good conversation with Dave's sister, Bobbe Jean. She had left many birthday messages, so I called back. Reminded her Dave did not like to talk on the phone anymore.

Old stories, tracing history. Funny, we have never met in person, but talk a couple of times a year and know each other. If we didn't live on opposite ends of the continent we would be good friends. We reminded each other how much he is like his mother, so sweet, giving, and extending to others.

She recalled a gathering, funeral, I think. She remembers him 'working the room,' spending real time with each person, sitting down to talk. I told her he has not changed. I reassured her: "He is my husband, I love him. I am not just his caretaker."

Which is a good thing for me. The stats on caretaker health and well-being are not too encouraging. So if I am not a caretaker but a loving wife, a care *giver*...those stats do not include me.

This idea of mine of trying to get into his head, to be more there with him, is mellowing me a bit. Because I am not there, I have no idea what my change of approach might be doing for him.

I had the strangest recollection. About how we cannot ever be in anyone else's head. He called me one day at work. I was working at a mutual fund agency in downtown LA. He said, "I took Dutch to the vet and had him put down because he had been staring at the wall for a long time."

He and Sherril, his previous wife, had raised Dutch from a puppy, and followed him to mega wins on the dog show circuit.

After they divorced, Dutch went to another family, and then came into our life four or five years later when the child in their household became asthmatic. Dave loved this dog; I liked him a lot.

When he called to say he had Dutch put down, I was not particularly sad, the dog had become old-age daft and was staring at walls. But a phone call? Where was I in this? Was he protecting me? I do not know the answer. Has he always been with himself only? It was the same thing when his mother died. He called me at work to let me know. It was not an expected thing, heat stroke.

I said, "I'll be there in an hour." He: "No, it's okay, you don't have to come home." I did not understand why he would not want my comfort? Well, of course, I went. He must have wanted me to be there. Or maybe not. Can we truly ever know another?

I don't recall reading that the personalities of Alzheimer people become even stronger in their primary traits than they had been, but in Dave's case, what he 'was' is more so, or at least not different. He is even sweeter and more generous, considerate than ever.

His life is still very much his own. I am here for him in order to keep ours lives running.

I do have fantasies of a fuller life, more independence, more freedom to go where I please, when I please, and as long as I please.

February 22, 2006

Floating. Floating stage. Never heard it mentioned, but it must be the tail end of acceptance.

I did not tell Dave until this morning he was going to the dentist. For a teeth cleaning. He worries and worries about any changes in our normal routine.

I told him around eight this morning. He was okay for a while, working on the mailings. But then started to fuss. Asking what was happening today. Several times, about a half hour apart.

He got dressed and was ready hours ahead of time. Then he started rummaging around in his office, looking for his driver's license. Came to me in the office and asked about it. I explained he didn't need it, I would be driving.

Film in a loop, repeats over and over.

Finally, I told him he doesn't need it because he won't be driving anymore except to go up for the paper and mail…and to take the trash up.

He: "Not going up to Rainey's?"

"No" has always been my hardest word.

I told him about crashing into the Buick, twice, told him twice. That if he couldn't manage the car in our driveway, I was worried about him being out on the road. I also mentioned Dr. Gillette had said he should not be driving.

Hurting those I love is the most painful thing for me.

෴

Ne me quitte pas
You drifting maple leaves of orange and reds
Brushed across the lawn in scattered order…
Tell to me that you will be here again
Next year
Tell me you will not leave me,
Ne me quitte pas.
Though remind me, maple drifting yellow that
Today is all
Remind me to look now…

We have this.

❦

I once cut open my wrist while opening a bale of hay, and feared bleeding out before I could get back to the house; another time I opened my knee catching a big and wild ewe, and once chopped off the end of a finger while pruning.

Nothing… bring it on. Pain any of my beloveds and I will rage. And so, today, his pain, his confusion. Over and over and over. "What are we doing, where we going?" Then back to the driver's license. Didn't he need it for the test, the driver's test? When we went to the insurance agent so he could check out the new car, Dave thought he was going for a driving test.

He must live a nightmare when things change.

All the way in to town it was the same thing. He recognized nothing. And asked the same question, four or five times…but did recognize the answer each time. Just couldn't hold it, make new memories.

I am so much more patient than six months ago and quietly repeated the answers.

When we got to the dentist, he had no idea where we were or what for. We have been with Pam, the hygienist, and Dr. Dumont for twenty years. They take good care of him.

I left him there to go to the Havurah to make the Newsletter corrections. The dentist's office people would call me when he was finished. And they knew with absolute clarity he was not to walk out the door.

Oh laws.

He was there. Just sitting. Waiting.

Chapter 16

FEBRUARY 24, 2006

We had one of our stranger exchanges while we were at the table working on mailings.

Dave, pointing to our blue sealer dots: "I need one of those, the thing that I put on my face."

I: "You mean your glasses? Why don't you look in the bathroom, maybe you took them off when you washed your eyes?"

He comes back with his toothbrush: "All I could find was my toothbrush; I've seen another one of them around."

As I am about to start looking, he points to rolls of stamps: "There are three of them over there."

What is happening in his head? Yesterday the dentist said he had been lucid, seemed to understand what was going on, talked about the sheep and llamas and made a joke about feeding the llamas candy bars.

One moment things are just out of his grasp, and the next he is able to reel it in for a while: we were listening to one of those elevator music stations. A new song started out with an incongruous drum clank.

I said: "What was that?" I was surprised, but only a little, that he had heard the same thing and replied: "I don't know, it sounds like someone tripped over one of those big metal feeders out in the barn."

That was exactly what it sounded like. He seems to have his music stuff in a special memory pod. I wish he would bring out his trumpet to play again. When I mention it he says, "I've done that." It is what he says when he means he has had a good go at something and isn't interested in returning to that phase of his life.

I think a lot these days about love. Not so much about love itself, whatever it is.

That love must surely be such a powerful emotion that we are molded by it and so our lives are determined by it.

I think about what it does, how it motivates and sometimes shackles.

What would be the cost of walking away from love, from those I love? Or one in particular. I would never walk from my children, my grandchildren.

What if I walked away from Dave? Took him down the street and said, "This is your home now." It is impossible. I do not know how bad it will get. I am ready for diapers and drooling. I am not ready for those eyes, those hazel and sometimes blue eyes to look at me and wonder who I am.

But hasn't he, completely involuntarily, walked away from me?

I am looking now out on the south pasture where a few of the sheep, a few of the llamas graze.

Do I love them? *No.* Do I love that there are animals and pastures? *Yes.*

Do I want to be constrained by others, environments even, because I love them? *No.*

Do I want Janis' world: *Freedom is just another word for nothing left to lose?*

Sometimes.

Do I ever drive the road by the airport without thinking, *I will just go...somewhere.* No.

I could wander the world by myself, but am afraid to drive to Ashland and back at night. One is traveling among people, easy to touch; the other, entirely alone…no lights, no *shoulders*.

Paris probably, just wander a bit, then come back home. Remembering when Dave and I wandered there. He and I trying to find a particular art place. My running behind a man asking, "Monsieur, monsieur, ou et le Poulet Vericoix?" Dave was impressed at my high school French, did not know after that I confused *a gauche* and *a droit*, left and right. So of course we were lost.

He depended on me even then, 1994. Well, I knew how to hail a taxi to get us out of that fix, but it was an adventure.

Looking back, I see that was the beginning of the beginning. He loved the adventure of new places, but was confused about where we were, or where we were going. The money exchange was beyond him. I was in charge. As always.

But I could do it, jump in a plane and go, wearing whatever. People seem to want to take me in, so I would get there perfectly intact. Buy clothes along the way. What a sublime adventure *that* would be!

Just me and *the kindness of strangers* (seems to be one of my favorite phrases these days.) A test. See if what I see in the mirror is what others see in me.

Well, that is *narishkeit*, foolishness. I know they do. There was this cool black porter at the Chicago Airport. I was outside for a smoke. He looked at me and said, "Hey, I like the way you dress, not trying to be something else." I loved the compliment…and that he was ok to say it.

Did I know that man, what he was saying, more than I know Dave now? Yes and no. When I wear all blue, shirt and jeans, he tells me he likes my colors. As with the music he always knows, another sense is strong for him…colors. He likes the colors of the stamps, of the food, and the sky.

How much of me does he see behind the colors of my jeans and shirt?

February 26, 2006

I am gathering memories. Might need them someday.

Eighteen months ago, summer of course, the hardest months out here, I knew we could not hang in for too much longer. A friend suggested a possibility of a place for us in Ashland. My druthers for where to go. He said it would be available in early 2007. I said, "Perfect, gives me two years, eight seasons, to say good-bye to here."

To gather the memories. To say: look at this peony, do not forget it. The way, last September, the pinkish cosmos stood just in front of the pinkish hydrangea, with the blue salvia as a foil. *Do not forget this.*

I took a picture, have taken many. The pictures are reminders. The real memory includes the light, the smell of the land around, the cats and dogs who have come to stay in the pack with me.

And the birds, so many these days, oblivious to our movements now that the trees are so tall, their habitats so secure. Just carrying on with their songs and squabbles, the demands of the fledglings for that last bit of food before they are forced out on their own.

We returned home from Eugene a couple of hours ago. Just this moment, I am listening to the Neil Young album Patrick and Katie gave me this morning. A quiet rain is just starting. Must have been a windy time the over-night we were gone because there are leaf packets from the roof all over the deck – another memory to save.

In one day, the forsythia bloomed. Missed the opening. One day. But hah, the King Alfred Daffodils, very pregnant, won't open until tomorrow. And I am here for it.

No first opening daffodil or forsythia can compare to hearing my son play the mandolin. He started learning it seven months ago.

This kid of mine. A whole person. The marvel of grown children—how much of their early being remains. Patrick's curiosity and ability to focus stood out. He was three when we took him to his first day of Montessori Pre-School, a room full of discoveries. Parents were encouraged to stay for a while. It was clear after only minutes that Patrick was in his element. We called across the room to say good-bye—he didn't even turn from his challenge, just gave a vague wave behind his back to indicate he had heard.

He is sitting on the couch. I in the big leather chair, Dave in the comfy smaller chair by the fireplace, Sparkie the Pom on his lap, Cindy at my feet. Patrick is wearing jeans, blue denim shirt. Wavy black hair, some grey coming in. That handsome face, becoming angular with maturity, forty-two now, wiry arms, hands and fingers now used to draw music from a mandolin. Trained as a trumpet player, much, very much different. But music is music to these lucky ones.

He was taught by Dave, the man in my life with the trumpet. Well, there are two men now. My husband and my son. Patrick crosses his legs, puts the strap over his neck. And starts to finger and pluck and strum. And this music comes out. This stuff that puts you back in very old, very old merrie England. This stuff that puts you straight into Appalachia.

After the recital we were on to the core of my question to him: What is it about music? We agree it is hard wired. He talked about his connection to Celtic music, mine to Semitic, the minor key pieces.

His genetic home is in the Celtic…and mine? I said, "Maybe I am really core Jewish." He shrugged. A shrug that said, "Maybe."

He is a scientist and an atheist. Also an involved member of their Unitarian Universalist congregation.

Strikes me funny I have been an atheist since I was about eighteen, raised my kids that way, and yet, now, three of the four of us are involved in religious communities. In Jennifer's case, hugely so.

Though she and I have not had God discussions in a long time, I do remember the conversation with Andrew, Jennifer's Rabbi husband, around their dinner table when he assured me it was not necessary to believe in God to be a Jew. Phew.

My take on it, last night in more conversation with Patrick, and right this moment, is the human mind is not capable of comprehending God, what it means to be omnipotent, omniscient. We really are not.

So, let's go *Tikkun Olaming (repairing the world)* because it just makes good sense. (Game theory, dontcha know.)

Not to mention the obvious, said many times: reality does not depend on my knowing it, and I do not have to believe in God for God to believe in me.

We went to his lab this morning. I had not been there in a while. My best painting, sixty small canvasses, is up, a major piece on the wall of his big office.

When I look at my kids and my grandkids, I fall in love with myself. I did good. Very good.

And in the mirror? Looking better each day.

Chapter 17

FEBRUARY 27, 2006

We were watching *Sense and Sensibility*. Jane Austen is so funny, and timeless. Emma Thompson portrays so perfectly Elinor's acceptance of her position.

I decided to come in to write, so asked Dave if he wanted to watch something else.

He: "Yeah, see what you can get, 'cats' in wigs make me nervous."

This guy was born hip. And these bits, his indelible vocabulary, help make our new life possible. The same jokes, the same maneuvers. The usual bit in the morning when he is working on the mailings and I come in regularly to check on him, as much for the sake of the business as for him. He becomes frustrated when he loses track of what he is doing, but he will survive a stamp in the wrong place; the business might not be as lucky if my boss gets impatient with sloppiness impacting her client base, so I check and re-check.

Sometimes I have just gotten out of the shower and do my five minute walk-through, not taking time for a robe.

I: "How are you doing, how is it going?"

He: "It's going just fine." Then, with the Groucho eyebrows: "It looks like you're going just fine too."

We are still surfing the same wave in so many ways. Just now, as every single night so it becomes funnier and funnier:

I have come to my office, Dave is watching TV. Cindy, my shadow, awakes to realize I am not in the room. She scratches at the door. Both of us, I in my office, he in the living room, get up to let Cindy through the door… We meet there with a laugh, "Once again." And Cindy chugs her little old self through the door, oblivious.

I have not lost him yet.

Today with Simone was sublime. Also with Kathy, here for the first hour, planning her business, using my computer. And back and forth, back and forth with this adored child.

Awed once again by love.

I was exhausted by our trip, the three hours to Eugene, driving up and back through the mountains for an overnight.

But I had everything I could want here today with Simone, and I needed to be there for her to make her time just as good as it could be, a cranky or tired grandma would not do.

We made muffins, then a cake. Built housing for the toy animals, drew, stickered, and pasted. Danced and bounced. And talked and talked. Helped her get the "th" sound so she can say "other" instead of "ahder".

Dave looks on with grandfatherly enjoyment, but she moves too fast for him now to follow. He loves to tell Kathy what an amazing child she is, so he is noticing something - I think he likes her athleticism.

Until now my greatest loss has been my grandmother. The moment she died, Thomas, Kathy, 20 months old, and I were in a rowboat on a lake in the Grand Titons. Grandma had been dying with the most amazing grace. That day, that moment, I felt it, I knew it was done. As soon as we got back to land, I called Mother. Yes, it was so, Grandma had just died.

She was the most generous, gracious, and beautiful lady, who touched everyone she knew with caring. You would have thought she was a queen, privileged to dispense favors at no cost to herself. Her influence on me was huge. I learned dispensing favors that come from caring have no cost, rather, unsought benefit. Her voice, her lessons how to live, are with me still. I was struck hard by her loss.

And she did not change when her circumstance did. She moved from the grand houses where she and Grandpa used to live to a tiny, tiny house on Gower after she married Jose.

Why she married Jose will ever remain a mystery to those of us still alive. Why she divorced Grandpa was clear to all of us. Damn womanizer. But they were forever friends. Odd. Well, not so odd if you ever met Grandma.

She had to go to work. She worked in a travel agency on Larchmont. And wore the same jewels she had always worn. She bequeathed me the pearl necklace with the sapphire clasp she wore to work. Can you imagine? Well, of course, what else does a grand lady wear to work?

I used to stop by on my way home from school to see her. The big welcoming smile. I was adored unconditionally. It is a special love grandmothers have no strings, no expectations.

It is a given. And now, I am her gift to Simone. A legacy whose value is above the treasured pearls.

February 28, 2006

I think it's time to take care of myself a bit. I see being a caregiver can take its toll, but I figured, knowing myself pretty well, that doing my duty, accepting my responsibility was, indeed, taking care of myself. Danger lurks in that way of thinking, thinking I need to take care of myself only once in a while.

The danger is that the needle on the gas gauge will slowly move from full to empty while I'm not paying attention. And, so, what happens when I am out of gas? When the wind stops, the ship stalls? It is stalling a bit now. I have no one to talk to. This man cannot communicate the difference between stamps and his glasses.

We never did discuss Kant's *Critique of Pure Reason*. That's okay, I had philosophy classes for that. Instead we had endless conversations about music, about our family histories, and about our future.

For weeks recently he was afraid of the hurricanes. Read the paper, heard the news. He could not place us on the map in his head relative to where they were taking place.

I want out. Out of the daft husband, out of the deaf dogs, the cat that pees in the attic. I want to spend the rest of my life with the living.

༄

I am not Wyeth's heroine
Who crawls the hill.
I crawl the pitted ground
The level, pitted ground
Of the ordinary.
Toward the ochre pasture,
The dimming sky.

༄

Or, alternately, with headphones on, listening to *Cavalera Rusticana* and reading about *chaos theory* and the *fabric of the cosmos*, while sunning under the apple tree and smelling the lilies.

Or, the buffet table at the Eden Roc Hotel in Cap D'Antibe (where I got my first bikini burn at age fifteen), seducing charming and smart widowers who know what the hell I am talking about! Well, actually, they would be seducing me.

Of course, there is the *'til death do us part* business. I am poor at rationalizing bad behavior. Still, one can imagine, play with possibilities, dream it.

I remember a woman in Torah class, a psychologist, saying that surviving spouses who live and thrive are those who accept and so move on.

I find myself so often saying, "Well, that's life," "Well, it can't be helped." "Oh well." "Whoopsie, it's ok, we'll fix that." Accepting what cannot be changed. Apparently, it keeps my gas tank over the empty line. And *the wind in my sails.*

Okay, enough about gas in tanks and wind in sails. My recovery comes from the breath of a new season. The daffodils are out. The frogs are in full chorus.

So, the beginning. Another year!

March 1, 2006

Ah, March. Don't I love it? My birth month. The daffodils. In my room as a child, my dresser was painted aqua, with daffodils on the face of the drawers. The space of my life between then and now can often seem vacant. By which I mean, as though there was nothing between the then and now.

But truly, it is filled with millions of bits.

Yesterday as Simone jumped into the house, little jump, by little jump, I explained *Xeno's Paradox* to her. The look, the smile, she gave. She wants to know what I am talking about.

I think my mother must have done well by me. I have until this moment thought, *I am the mother, the grandmother I am because I wanted to improve upon her mothering.*

I am wrong. She really did the best she could. My turn now.

March 2, 2006

Walking through the room to check on him, I said: "Pretty nice party we had today."

He: "I was just about to say that to you: Some were new; some had been here for past performances."

Now, if that is not a clue to what is going on in there, I am not paying attention. There were no "some" here, only Beth and Kathy, my best friend Beth and our daughter Kathy. He greeted Beth with his usual, "Hi, sister, how are you. It's been a long time." True, it had been.

Kathy's arrival surprised him a little. Not the usual morning visit with Simone in tow. But he sees a party in any gathering. We were always the last to leave a party.

I'm guessing that to him, every event is *new*. However, he recognizes those who were here for "past performances."

At lunch, he was in the conversation, but with his own special take on it. When the word 'vet' was mentioned, as in veterinarian, he told us of his positive experience with the post-Korean War benefits for returning vets. His being able to continue college. About his basic training and being selected to be in a band to entertain the troops.

Before Beth left, I asked her how he seemed to her. She thought he was in good shape. Better than in some previous times. She suggests he has ups and downs, as we all do.

What I see is sleep and stress are the most important variables. When he has enough sleep and is not worried, preoccupied with events he knows not of, he is as on top of it as he was two years ago.

What I am learning is not to tell him something stressful is going to happen (e.g. the dentist) until the last minute. And the good things? I let him know far ahead of time when there something to look forward to.

He was looking forward to seeing Beth; knows her, likes, her, and, as she pointed out, he does not have to leave his safe environment.

Neither do I. Yet.

Chapter 18

March 3, 2006

It seems our cat Briquette has decided, or defaulted, to die in the attic. She is not dead yet, but unless she allows me to rescue her, she will be soon. I have brought her down a couple of times today and yesterday, standing on the ladder, reaching to the eaves, standing on the washing machine, coaxing her. This evening she only stares.

Picking up a cat can be scary; bringing one down from above, precarious. She is terrified, claws out grabbing at whatever she can reach. First the beams, then my arms and chest.

She no longer can see her way down to the top of the freezer... or is afraid to jump in the way she has for the last ten years. Another of the creatures in my life has gone coo-coo.

I am going to let her go. Put up a bowl of water, but will not feed her up there. I just cannot manage a cat living for years in the attic and having to climb every day onto the washing machine. Never mind the hygiene.

Never mind the glitches; there is little I would change in my adult life. These thirty years with Dave. I embrace them despite this nasty end.

Yesterday, my naughty boy llama, Dempsey, spit at me at close range, packing my hair with alfalfa. In truth, I got a bigger charge out of that than seeing the *Mona Lisa*. Seeing the *Winged*

Victory at the end of the hall in the Louvre is another story. A burst of joy. And my first opera: *La Traviata*. Those arias sent me soaring.

I go back and forth in this, these life affirming moments and times, to make clear to myself there are many moments, even now, that will spin in my memory. Give me bursts of joy, make me feel alive, happy to be alive.

Dave's illness has not at all taken that from me. How could it? What he is going through is not something directed at me. To wallow in victim-hood would be my choice, not his blame.

I choose not to wallow.

March 4, 2006

Winter Shabbats are the best for me because I can really rest. When it is warmer, the garden demands attention no matter what day it is.

I cannot seem to shake this weariness. Perhaps it is because I haven't been sick in a long time. My sicknesses always mean my body and soul need a break.

So I'm taking an easier way out. Sitting in the chair looking north, reading a good book, today John Irving's *Until I Find You*, is the perfect medicine.

A real bonus today has been Dave's ability to work on the mailings without much help. It has been increasingly irritating to be constantly interrupted by him and the animals. Like taking a hike and tripping over a twig every ten feet. Often I feel like squawking, "Leave me alone for just one hour!"

That would be impossible with Dave who is always apologetic when he needs to ask for help or direction. Especially if I am at the computer. I suppose he imagines I am working. The animals are another story: they do get my ire sometimes.

We rescued the cat after all. When she was desperate to come down, I was able to reach her pretty easily by climbing on top of the upright freezer and folding her in my arms to bring her to safety. Well, my safety anyway. Even if I weren't sure to be overloaded with guilt if I left her there to die, how could I explain it without seeming like a monster?

Actually, those who know me well would understand perfectly and haul me off to the loony bin, sure I had gone 'round the bend for real this time. "Michelle, letting an animal die if she could prevent it? No, wrong woman, she's clearly beside herself."

Does that happen to people, they go crazy when they can't cope anymore? Maybe that's what a nervous breakdown is. More and more I fantasize about how it would be to live alone. I never have, going straight from my parents' home, to a college dorm, to marriage.

This John Irving book is filled with his usual odd characters and improbable events, all underscored with a certain inevitability and pathos. It begins with the boyhood of the main character. This line on the book jacket strikes me and makes me sad: "In this way, in increments both measurable and not, our childhood is stolen from us not always in one momentous event but often in a series of small robberies, which add up to the same loss."

In spite of my complaints about my parents, my childhood was not in the least stolen. In fact, even the egregious behavior of my stepfather could not stop me from being happy and glad of life. And even that relationship had many pluses. He certainly reinforced my good opinion of myself: smart, capable, responsible, and attractive.

The enduring problem has been the fear and resentment I feel for dominant, authoritarian men, fear and resentment made worse by my first husband. I've also been left often torn between an urge to be judged, hoping for approval, and the desire to withdraw from social contact.

March 5, 2006

At my window beat
Images of time and death
Curious, I look.

I am thinking about ironies, how I love them.

A few hours after I brought Briquette down yesterday, she went back. For the life of me, I cannot figure out how she is getting up there. I have made barricades with cardboard boxes, piled on every possible platform she could be using to launch herself at the drywall and onto the attic ledge.

This morning around five, she started yowling. I put another pillow over my head, no sympathy whatever. Then later, when she sounded serious, I went up again. Unfortunately, she was off position just a little so she had to grab my face, sinking her claws into my lip.

The most marvelous irony for me would be to die because of some mishap with one of the animals. Having loved and protected animals my whole life that might even be considered a tragedy: a character flaw resulting in my own demise. It will not be cat claws in the face that would do it, unless I fell off the freezer and cracked my skull on the cement. More likely to be caused by falling over one of the dogs in the dark, breaking a hip, then getting pneumonia. Or being bashed in the head by a ram while picking hay off the ground.

Oh never mind tragedy, this would be a farce!

I often think of my own death. My grandmother died at 64, only a year and a half older than I am now. There is a certain curiosity about it. *Will that big lumber truck suddenly veer into my lane and hit us head on? Will one of our hunter neighbors lose control and send a bullet zinging my way? Will I indeed fall off the freezer?*

Dave would not know what to do. Even if he remembered about 911, our phone line is always tied up with the internet and he does not know how to use the cell phone. Well, those things can be worked out. Maybe we should practice emergency responses. (Just checked, he doesn't always remember the address, so we'll just have to free up the land line so the call can be traced.)

Then what would happen to him? It is too soon for a care facility, but he could not live alone. Even with a day person coming in, he might wander off and get lost. Locking him in would be too dangerous—he could start a fire and not be able to escape, or he might panic by being trapped inside.

I better check these things out before I try to rescue the cat again. Surely there are solutions. Oh I'll think about that tomorrow.

Chapter 19

MARCH 6, 2006

Art leads.

We hadn't seen the Academy Awards in a long time. I was impressed by the serious movies that were put up for the kudos.

Artists grab; are not constrained. We are not going to let go. We want to speak of what has not been spoken of before. Building, however, on the work of those who have taken chances before us.

Could I be speaking of my life if Virginia Wolfe, Vita Sackville-West, Charlotte Perkins Gilman, May Sarton, had not before me?

The artists are our real salvation. It is amazing to me the courage that is out there. Although we still live in a world where artists like Theo van Gogh can be murdered because of their work, the courage I refer to is the personal courage required to expose oneself. I do this because I want the intimacy that comes from being known by another. I also want to touch others with my story, to provide hope.

I just finished talking to my younger sister, Barbie. Her 57th birthday yesterday. She talked of being overwhelmed by the sadness in the world, the pleas for support that come her way. I suggested she take one or two causes and let the rest of the sadness be only filtered in. Most of us do what we can in our small ways.

I do believe there is a way out still, a way of rescuing the planet and human civilization, though I have doubts, when I see pictures of women encased in black, covering even their faces.

But then, Simone pulls me from my gloom by coming over tonight for a rehearsal in preparation for her stay with us while Kathy is at a conference in Atlanta. She takes me into our room where she will sleep with me, peeling off her clothes, "I sleep naked. Tell me a story. It will get dark because it is bedtime."

March 8, 2006

Oh laws, I feel as though I am raising twins. A quick girl and a slow boy.

They got into it today. Simone was sitting on the couch with the bag of chips, which she had purloined from the lunch table. I thought I had made sure Dave had enough. Apparently not.

As happens with these wonderful inevitabilities, I was talking with Kathy on the cell phone. She had a break in her conference. It happened so fast that we all are trying to play it back.

Dave needed more chips so went over to get the bag from Simone. She resisted. He grabbed and yelled. She screamed, gave it up, and dropped her glass of water.

I screamed, apparently tossed the phone so I could accost him, yelling, "What the hell do you think you are doing? How dare you?" Actually whacking at his chest I was so angry.

He backed off, I comforted Simone, and she let off sniffling. I then realized Kathy was hearing all of this through the phone that was on the floor over by the fireplace.

My heart in Atlanta, now worrying for my daughter. My heart in Sam's Valley, fearing damage to my granddaughter.

And later to my sweet Dave. Over and over, all afternoon, he wants to recap what happened. He doesn't know the why or the wherefore. He is so sorry, apologizes to Simone without my urging.

And so, I am depressed on this dreary day. This earth mother inclination is a burden again. Wanting to flee again. Waiting to fly.

But now as I write, Kitty Rings is nudging my elbow, and I smile. And Simone will be back here soon after a few hours with Roxy, her 'other' mother.

We will play crazy music. And ballet music. She will dance. I will video it. And so remember, something to try to remember, when my own mind is also perhaps gone.

March 9, 2006

Two children taken care of, for now. One in the living room watching *Law and Order*, the other in my bedroom watching *Princess Bride*.

Kathy doesn't want her to watch the torture scene. I thought I was monitoring, but checked just as it was on. She averred she knew it was make believe and wanted to watch it. Well, it was short.

This child of mine, my only granddaughter, Simone Claire Carnahan Darice.

The hours that Kathy and Roxy... and I, spent poring over the 'pedigrees' of potential sperm donors. Kathy was to be the birth mother, the milk mother. The decision had yet to be made, so the search was still on.

Roxy had a son, Sean, who died after only a few hours. She was reluctant to risk a repeat. But willing, wanting a child. We had all the information, histories, of these men. How tall, what color eyes, what color skin, education, family history of illness, etc.

We toyed with romantic ideas of mixed races, falling in love with heritage, our guessing the potential results of the combination of genes. The concern was for the child brought into the society in already tenuous circumstances, the child of lesbians.

(When Jennifer and Andrew considered adopting after many years of infertility, I suggested there were more black children available. Jennifer said she could not handle being a mother to a boy who many people were afraid of. What a horrible reality.)

The selection was finally made. We heard his voice on a tape the clinic sent. Wishing them well. It was a nice voice. Genuine.

And, boy, we sure got her! A perfect child, a perfect prize.

Another irony in a life full of them: Simone was conceived the year Dave was diagnosed. How odd—it is as though she is growing to fill the spaces he is leaving behind. Not in my love, but in the small joys of each day.

March 10, 2006

Well, the jury's back. I am making myself crazy. I have suspected this for a while, but today it really hit.

It is true I walk at least a mile each day Simone is here, attending to her needs as well as those of Dave, the animals and myself. It is true I sometimes become tense, harried, and feel put upon. However, insisting I adhere to some standard of performance in the other part of my life makes for my own crazy making.

I have become nearly obsessed with clearing my desk and having the office in order by Friday night, Shabbat. I want to wake up Saturday morning completely free. No nuisancey jobs undone.

So instead of facing it may not be possible this week with Simone as my houseguest, I took on a postcard mailing for my boss: Sandy's most recent sale. Today it involved some re-formatting for a new type of card stock bought by mistake. Waste the paper? Not me.

It just hit me: "I do not need to be doing this today, let alone right now."

Dropped it and went out to play with Simone and be patient with Dave.

Chapter 20

March 14, 2006

Well, it has been a very good day…it is Jennifer's birthday, I got a speeding ticket, and I spent an hour and a half in the dentist chair.

First with the speeding ticket. This is a clue, as if I don't have others, that I need to get out and mingle instead of relying on instant gratification. Social gratification is an emolument.

This new little car is really peppy. Her choice is 80 mph. Who am I to refuse a Beemer? Never having had a luxury car before, (though many I have loved; actually my '64 Continental was pretty special though old) I am not sure of the rules to ordering favorites.

Well, the OHP man coming the other direction thought there were rules. Rules *I* should adhere to. It was so exciting; he ripped a U-turn and flashed his lights.

"Ma'am, I clocked you at 78 mph." *Dang, my speedometer must be off; I thought I was going eighty.*

I was charming, he was sweet. I indeed was going too fast; deer, squirrel and such could be in the road.

He said, "And we see beeves on the road sometimes too."

I was incredulous, "Beavs?" *I am thinking, what would beavers be doing out here. I didn't know we had beavers in the area, let alone on the road.*

He: "Beeves, cattle sometime get on the road."

I worked hard not to break out laughing.

He knocked it down to 75 mph, said it would save about $100. And, if I went to court, it would be reduced even further.

Jeeze, how much would I pay not to have to go to find parking at the Courthouse? Fifty bucks sounds reasonable.

The dentist, not so bad, just rummaging and fixing, another trusted man in my life. Lots of teeth work in the last couple of years. "Gettin' old's not for sissies", as they say, *nor is it cheap.*

Dave's mouth is simpler; he just keeps losing them in spite of his regular cleanings. Why do they bother with x-rays? They're falling out. He won't tolerate appliances, let alone a bridge.

Let the teeth fall where they may.

And so, now, Jennifer's birthday. One of the highlights of my life.

Such a pregnancy. Such a wanted child. I went straight from my OB's exam with the positive results to Magnin's for maternity clothes. Spend $200 on gorgeous clothes. Can't even imagine how much 1966 dollars are worth today.

I was twenty-three, full of life. Being a mother is the best of me. Being a grown up, in the new world of the-wife-of-a-lawyer, a socially responsible joiner of leagues, was not as much fun. Except for the cocktail parties.

The trade off was staying in school, never stopping.

This day, March 14, 1967, lying on the table, the doctor saying, "Well, do you want boy or girl?"

I: "Another girl would be nice."

He: "We like girls too. Ah ha! This is what you have."

She was angry at having been brought out. Screamed and screamed. Everyone in the room was smiling. She is so perfect, purple because of the oxygen, at the top of the viability scale.

Nothing has changed. Another perfect daughter

March 16, 2006

Every bone and muscle in my body aches, but I feel so good. Funny how when younger I could feel so good without all the aches and pains.

Finishing the newsletter, a good one, is such a kick. An "Ah, YES!"

And cleaning house for Patrick and Katie's arrival. Some garden spiff up, though not so much to do in March. Good job, Missy.

Processes are a pleasure, but the standing back, looking at the product, is the ultimate reward. Well, I don't know, have to get back to you on that one.

Same in the garden, I love the working, but the seeing it done, or at least one of the jobs done, is the reward. The garden is never done. Of course not, things grow.

I wonder if this is how God feels. *"Okay, I put this Michelle here with these parents, threw in some siblings, and gave her a lot of good stuff, beauty, brains and breeding. Laid a few traps just to see how she would take it. Ah, hey, she did okay. So I think I will move her up a notch. I'll let her take care of her baby sister, Kathy. And protect her little brother Chip. Love and care for my animals.*

If she meets these challenges, she will graduate to teacher and caregiver. Not of the world, that is my job, but of hers.

Okay, good job Michelle. Now go out and do what you have learned."

I reply: "Yes sir, I know my place. A couple of complaints here and there. I'll bet I could do a better job if I could sing, but thanks for the dancing part, I'm a dynamite dancer. Brunette is fine, but in my heart I am a redhead, Rhonda Fleming. Not Rhonda Fleming, Rhonda Fleming's hair."

When I was ten, I saw her playing tennis at Charlie Farrell's club near our house in Palm Springs. Well, of course, a ten year old stripling would want to be that goddess.

A few weeks before it had rained frogs…I know now it was emerging frogs, not frogs raining. I was wandering around The Racket Club by a big cistern. It was pouring rain and tiny frogs were blanketing the ground.

"So, God, was this another of my tests? Or my future? Dumping me into the plague of the frogs? Well, of course you knew I would not be afraid of frogs, only fascinated."

But again, and again: where the Hell was my mother? How was it this child was alone there? Maybe a good thing all this freedom to roam and learn for myself?"

It is problematic to posit a "God" now. Not at all what I was thinking as a child. I was alive with discovery. Getting up early, before anyone else, slipping on a one piece bit of sunsuit, no underwear, and just getting out into the day. Jumping into life, as children do.

Dave's childhood was so different. A cohesive family, though a tyrant father. He says they got into all kinds of mischief while his dad was away. But even with the dad there, they created a family band, all musicians, all support for one another. The mom cooking, weaving his sisters' wedding gown fabric.

Nothing what I experienced with absent parents. Mother's idea of connecting to me was asking me to change her purses, swap the contents of one into the other before she went out.

Thomas also had very present parents, though slightly daft. They supported me continually through all of our marriage and divorce. They agreed Thomas was slightly nuts.

This could all be my imagination of course, memories filtering through fifty years. The holding on to old grudges.

She did the best she could, my mother.

Alzheimer Diary

March 17, 2006

I am losing him again. This morning he was depressed. He was actually able to say so when I asked if anything was wrong.

I try to find out what he is thinking. He may have worries I can relieve. He worries so before the fact. But then, many of us do.

I did not tell him until this morning Katie, Patrick and Grant were coming tomorrow. So maybe that was it, his fear of changes and disruption of our routine. We have been house cleaning the last few days so he might have had a clue before now. The only time we clean house is when someone is coming.

He kept questioning me, "So it is the whole family." I reminded him Alex would not be here. He is on a coming of age project in Portland.

It has always been a bit painful to me, I can hardly call it a sorrow, though that word did come to mind, that he does not, and has never, said "*My* daughter, my son, my grandchild." It is always "Michelle's."

He has been a remarkable stepfather. He does love the children, and they love him even more.

I am trying to remember the color of the chair, I think it was white. Against the window in our house in Arcadia. We had just recently become a family. I see Dave sitting in the chair with eleven-year-old Patrick in his lap. My son now has a loving father rather than a perpetually angry one.

Kathy was glad to be rid of the old father, but understandably suspect of the new one, even though she had known him since she was three. It was not about him. She was fourteen. Need I say more?

Just nine, Jennifer went with the flow. Didn't much like her father either. This new constellation was so mellow.

I hate this so much. My man is gone. What is here is another child. Hah, what irony. I do so love children. Those perfect innocents, teaching me. To me, the supposed teacher, they are whispering: listen, listen, listen.

A cosmic joke coming into my life: a baby, Simone, and an old man, another baby. I think I get it.

So cool, I got it. Now do *I* get some juice? *Well lady, this is the juice.*

∽

*Tonight
Like a Bruegel painting,
The fields, ochre, mauve and moss
The sky blanched, not quite blue
Remind me of you.*

*You who are now faded
Faded like this twilight.*

*Will I remember you
As you were
When the sun was rising?
The fields were pink instead?
When you were rising not from grayness
But from my bed?*

∽

Chapter 21

MARCH 18, 2006

I had a terrible dream this morning. I was climbing up a ladder into an attic. A man came and pulled the ladder away. I hung onto the edge of the attic opening as he tried to pull me down. I kicked and kicked at his face.

I awakened because I was kicking at my own ankles.

What do I think the dream means? An attic is a place to hide. Not the same as running away. Who is the man? Not Dave. Someone or something bad. The disease? My obligation?

MARCH 19, 2006

It truly is only family that loves you.

Dogs, of course, stay with you also. Friends are occasions for learning about yourself and your humanness. And maybe you care enough if they care back. Or maybe you say, "I'd rather be with my peonies." But they come and go. I leave them, they leave me. Some special few become family.

Family love is not contingent. This is my experience.

Tomorrow is my birthday. I just got a jazzy music card from my sister: *Let's get together and celebrate.*

We have danced and danced so often. At the Marc Antony, Ashland Hills Inn, at Jasmine's. We danced in a Pub in Pasadena on

St. Patrick's Day. Hours under an umbrella on the patio, drinking beer forever on that bright sunny day. We stayed into the evening to dance with men who seemed charming, all the while knowing we would go back again soon to less exciting lives.

Kathy and I are the two people in the world who know each other best. My baby sister is one of my true loves. We know all the shit of our lives. And the good stuff. Without these kinds of loves, you are sentenced to be lonely and to take refuge in the emerging daffodils and the smell of the lilacs, if indeed they come out this year at all.

I am very sad. I am alone.

I just went out to fix Dave dinner. He asked what I was doing.
I: "Writing my diary."
He: "That must be interesting. Are you telling the truth?"
I: "Oh yes."
Would I cry for a lie?

MARCH 22, 2006

A few nights ago I dreamed Dave built me a structure of some kind: three boards across, a panel. Or maybe a trellis if it were much taller, or up-ended, much wider.

Soon after we moved here, we got an old truck. 1967 GMC. He constructed the most amazing stock rack. The back gate was the work of a craftsman: a solid panel with a carved out gate complete with hinges and hasp. It was a complex piece of carpentry, and perfect for hauling sheep

I don't think too much about what he can no longer do, at least not until I write of it. But it is there, there in my dream.

Grab one from the pen and close the gate; load the sheep, close the gate. Load another, and another, and another, and another. One time we did eleven. Into the pens, grab the lamb, lug him to the truck. Up the ramp, into the truck, onto the auction.

Each one of them to be killed.

It truly makes me sick—that I had the joy of the lambs and then killed them. What the hell was I thinking? Where did I lose myself? I am not leaving here until every one of my remaining sheep die of natural causes. Forget being realistic.

MARCH 23, 2006

I have been thinking all day about how I slid into a hobby that involves killing innocent creatures. Never will I forget that face, that look of the lamb we off loaded onto the auction ramp. The other ten went down, but this one stopped and looked back at us. Beautiful Lincoln ram lamb, black and silver, curls to his hocks. He was one of the most friendly. When and how did my heart harden to accept commerce more than life? Pride, power, ambition?

I wanted to be part of saving the Lincoln breed. To create the best, the beautiful. This was considered a rare breed, but that became important to me only later. I loved them. Majestic, smart, independent. The most incredible wool, coarse curls, lustrous and soft. Prized by weavers and a joy to spin, the wool dyed into a glow of color.

Ashland, 1984, a spinning group: I said I wanted to raise wool sheep, sheep that would not be killed for meat. The group was silent.

It was later I learned that if one needs to limit flock size, all but the best of the ram lambs will have to go. Usually neutered unless a good breeding prospect, then sold for meat. Or butchered on our farm and sold. We had no trouble selling, or eating the most delicious home grown lamb. In our early years, the best dinners were those when everything on our plate was homegrown, the veggies, the salad greens, the potatoes, and the meat.

It took a long time for me to recognize the ruthless truth that if I were to continue to eat meat, I would have to accept that what is on my plate was once alive. I still believe the animals butchered here on the farm were the luckiest of those eaten because before the slaughterer came they were in the barn, eating the grain they love. Then, pop, they were dead. No fattening yards, no being muscled around by uncaring cowboys. No trucks.

But then as our flock grew, there was the truck. Our truck. Taking them to auction. And who knows what happened after that? Some do. I don't want to think of it.

Our mission statement of Rock Creek Sheep was to create the best Lincolns we could. That was the fun part. Adding new genes to the flock, beautiful ewes, the ram you hope has the right stuff for the improvement you want: fleece, size, confirmation, head, and temperament.

Then you take your babies into the show ring, their fleece to the wool show. We had so many ribbons I threw them out as clutter. The major trophies are collecting dust on top of the bookcase.

The sheep we 'created' have their lineage out there in the show ring still, doing what we had hoped. Big strong tall lovable sheep: blacks, whites, silvers and variegated, absolutely gorgeous Lincolns.

We have still five boys and two old girls. Reminders.

I really think I would give it all up in order not to see the face of that little ram on the auction ramp.

Chapter 22

MARCH 24, 2006

If I didn't know I am okay, I would be worried about me too; Kathy was for a moment this morning.

My kids and Beth, see something here on the property, the house, as I only do on a wish list. A place in need of attention.

The worst room, Dave's office, was taken care of a couple of months ago. Patrick re-floored and painted, and bought a futon for a guest bed.

Three other rooms have the original, cheap, now cracking and lifting, vinyl tiles. Plus mud ugly: the kitchen, my office, and the guest room.

So today, Kathy and I went to Lowe's to pick out flooring. I absolutely abhor shopping. Big stores overwhelm me. Though once there, I can get caught up in the minutia. Kathy was surprised I followed through after having canceled yesterday with some excuse or other.

She is my guide, leads me to the right place, to meet Ryan, our person in flooring. We start with the kitchen: laminate or vinyl? Pergo or Armstrong? Color, design, boards ending at the same place or off set? They are both very patient. Kathy talks about decorating points I know not of. I ask her where she learned the fine points of decorating. Being an artist does not tell you about the floor not being the center of attention, just the base, etc, etc, etc. She watches decorating shows. *Good gravy.*

At some point I call for a chair. This is too much stimulation. Not to mention that I have not recovered from racing with Simone up the driveway on Wednesday. (I am better at sprinting, she at endurance.) We flip through the sample boards, weighing color (especially), type, and life, something about stain mastering.

I start to laugh. This seems the most ridiculous thing I have done in years. It is a giggle laugh, and then turns to crying, and back to laughing. Kathy: "Mom, are you all right? Are you all right? I'm worried about you."

I am all right. I tell her how out of the ordinary, *my* ordinary, I see my life when I read sections of Diary. It is these moments I will record and find absurd. My mother told me many times how she could tell what I was feeling by looking at my mouth. Now it is no longer only my mouth that gives me away. Laughing and crying sitting in a chair (no one else in the whole huge store was sitting in a chair), might have given me away to someone. Perhaps another person, wandering by, who now, tonight at this moment, is about to have a cat jump on her lap, smiled and recognized that state.

There is freedom in this for me now – the freedom that comes from not caring what a stranger thinks.

Not so much freedom when I was so frightened of Thomas. Though I drove for what I wanted, believed in, anxiety shook me most of the time. The stakes were so much higher then. My children. He threatened to take them from me. Powerful egomaniacal, paranoid bastard.

And I was ashamed of my weakness, my powerlessness.

But I drove on. Kept taking my classes. The worst time of embarrassment was handing out questionnaires for my research project. Stuart Fishoff's class. My hands shook as I passed the papers to each class member. But I did it, I did it.

After Thomas and I separated, I went to open my own bank account. I could barely write for shaking. Went to Robinson's to buy Jennifer shoes, could hardly sign. The sales girl looked at me peculiarly.

Hey, it is no wonder I am out here. With a man who doesn't question. And, just simple folks, the farmers who live out here. They hunt, drink beer, drive trucks and would save me in a minute. Assessments not necessary.

March 25, 2006

We just had an exchange I knew would come someday. There seems to be more than one stage of denial. At each plateau, and they are long, I think, *Okay, maybe it will stay this way and he will die of a heart attack instead.*

For months, I have been irritated when I say something to him, some observation of mine and he says: "Oh." I have finally grasped he is unresponsive because he does not understand what I have said. He hears the words, but they do not meaningfully come together for him.

Just now he came back into the living room wearing not only his down vest over his turtleneck, but his heavy robe. I told him I realized it was getting cold and I had turned up the heat. He looked at me blankly. Not connecting his garb with the chill of the room. Or that I was fixing the problem. I accosted him, repeating, "I have turned up the heat because I see you are cold." He still looks at me blankly. I gesture with the same ingathering arms I use for the blessing of the candles, trying to elicit something. "You could thank me." He: "Thank you." He has no idea for what.

He requires a lot more help with the mailings. Cannot see the end result. But is at sixes and sevens if he does not have work to do. I am starting to see this may get brutal. He hands me the funnies while I am engrossed in a book. Does not understand I do not want them now. Lays it on my shoulder. I just want to scream: "Go away, do not be considerate, why would you put the paper on my shoulder?"

Oh, my little man. I have lost you for most of the time. But not all.

We laughed over something this morning, a true good laugh. Mostly now, he does not remember our old jokes, the allusions. So they are trapped in my memory only.

༺ ༻

I would give you my heart of rubies
If you would give me yours
I gave you my heart of rubies
Yours spilled, scattered

༺ ༻

I wonder, again today, if these old sheep around here (some, unfortunately, not so old) are another test for me. When I start mowing down sheep, harden my heart, will I do the same to him? Cast him off into the care of others?

Telling his doctor, at the beginning of the disease, and also the finance guy, that I intended to take care of him myself, was not met with much reinforcement. Over and over I am asked how I am doing. Of course also, how he is doing. It does scare me a little. "They" seem to know something I don't but am getting a glimpse of. This is not just about love, which I recall only now in memories… and, today, looking at his hands. So nice and efficient, always the same clean with clipped nails. Strong, compact. A trumpet player's hands, a lover's hands. And a barn builder's, a sheep loader's, a tractor driver's. Not so much a weeder's.

It *is* about love. More and more though, it is the *Until death do us part*.

March 26, 2006

When we came to look at this place after three discouraging months spent searching for a rural property, we fell in love with it instantly. The drive down the driveway was all it took.

It must have been difficult for the owner, Mrs. Reed, to have me ask several times, "How can you leave here?" She patiently repeated, "It's time." Her husband had died a year or two before. She stayed. I truly know why she stayed. Perhaps also a glimmer of a clue, why she left. But only a glimmer, as yet.

My absolute druthers at this moment: stay, stay. The daffodils are extraordinary this year. A good sign of a long spring. Where else would I know this? I fanaticize doing what Mrs. Reed did, be here alone for a year, two. And then, perhaps say, "It is time."

My entry yesterday showed me something. Enough so that when Kathy came this morning, I told her I was seriously considering re-carpeting all the rooms…looking to the possibility of selling one day. The price is too high if we do not pay attention to the possibilities. So I must be thinking, *enjoy for now, because it will happen.*

The easiest way to explain was to print out what I had written last night and show it to her. She was absorbed, and a little struck, and sad. Feeling sorry for me. I was actually surprised. I live this every day. Others find it harder for me than I do myself.

Hey, I am woman, I am strong. Or not.

Last night's sleep was so deranged. The terrible dreams again. What a crazy thing to do for Shabbat: Finish an utterly absorbing book A THREAD OF GRACE, Mary Doria Russell, about the Italian partisans, the Catholic priests, Sisters, who protected and saved 50,000 Jews during Hitler's onslaught. The sacrifice of an incredible number of civilians. Oh, so many good. They did not give up their Jews. Not so many know this story.

And then later, watching the incredibly intense movie *Breaking the Waves* about the power of love and self-deception a true tragedy and tragic story. Even Dave was completely rapt. Two and a half hours of tension, attention.

So of course my dreams would be about inviting into my mother's house two people without necks to stay in the guest room. Then to find out they, the neckless people, had actually slept in my parents' bed and put huge stains on the mattress pad. Big blots of blue and purple, like bruises. My parents were coming back soon, so I had to wash it, leave no clues those people had been here, or that I had done something wrong.

I implored my cousin Dawn to go up the block to Robinson's to buy a new mattress pad. Faster than washing. But then, I went also, but couldn't find a parking place, or the place where I was to get on the plane to go again to Paris.

I awoke not having slept well, so relieved none of this was true. Or, only partly, perhaps: lost? guilty?

March 27, 2006

I just curled my lip at myself. Really did it. My viscera responding to something or other, that I don't like about me. I don't like that I sometimes respond to our changed life as though I am the victim. Sure, I take care of him in many ways. Feeding, protecting, nurturing, elevating, humoring, understanding (or attempting to), etc, etc… Aren't I grand? Surely I had more compassion another time.

This morning when he asked what day it is, and I responded, Monday.

He: "What day on the calendar" I: "Monday." He: "How soon is Christmas?"

"This is March 27th. Christmas is a long way away."

Later this afternoon he was stressed. Easy to see. He looked tired. I asked him about it. He said he is stressed. I ask about what. He: "I think it is because I don't sleep well." Of course the circle he does not see is coming: "Why do you think you don't sleep well?" He: "Because I am stressed."

I work gently to encourage him to tell me about what stresses him. Reassure him that Christmas, and visitors, are not coming soon. Finally, I hurt for him. And, to turn a circle again, this hurting will make it all the harder for me, my defenses down, my warrior mode erased.

Where is the silver bullet? The magic wand? The *just right* decision: Yes, Now! I want it Now! I keep waiting and waiting for a clue. Maybe this was it. It *is* a burden – maybe it's time to share it.

I looked today on MLS at houses for sale in Ashland. We are not priced out of possibilities. But I need to get to the core of my own question: can I trade this land for people? How long before the social me will mourn the alone me, the land, the coyotes, the daffodils? How soon would the trade prove too demanding, too inconsequential, too boring, even?

How many Havurah meetings will I go to, how many movies, plays, art walks, Thursday summers at the Bandshell, before I say: "Hey you know what, I don't give a damn?"

How long before I want my sheep, my spirea, my Corkscrew Willows. My hooting owls. My diving hawks and cruising vultures? The squabbling finches in the feeders? The elk, the deer, the quail.

I would be walking into the abyss of a relinquished dream. Over and over, I have looked out on the garden, the pasture, the sky with the rainbow and said: I am not leaving here. Will I prove myself a liar?

Chapter 23

March 28, 2006

Tonight, a perfect storm rages outside. Very exciting. The big flock of daffodils in the bed outside the front window, twenty year olds, are acting like three year olds. They are waving in the wind and rain, faces turned to me, imploring: I am the one, I am the one, or take a bunch of us, but be sure to take me, take me. They are adorable. But of course, I only give up my comfort for a flower in distress when the weather is fine. Well, sort of.

The real deal is the storm. Maybe there it is something about our reactions to ion balances, or whatever. Whatever the reason, I had a couple of surges of that *oh joy* feeling today. My own *Ode to Joy*. It balances out the other.

༄

Blow you crazy wind
Break the branches, uproot the weeds
You will not down me

I rage against you
We'll see who is the power
You, force. I have love.

༄

I have been irritated by two friends, younger than I, who suggest they are old. It is perfect nonsense. I might, perhaps, be old at eight-five.

They have forgotten how to be excited. Are so reconciled to their state. For crying out loud women, wake up! My dear friend Beth camps in Death Valley every couple of years (in a tent no less) and she is seventy. Skis even, with knee replacements (which she is not supposed to do, naughty girl.)

Excitement for life is still with me and means something about freedom, my teeth in the meat of life: flying down the road in my little Beemer, if I could have been sure of a clear road between Table Rock and Hwy. 62, I would have gone 100. The car manual says not to go faster than 108 before 25K miles. So, I sort of have permission being as how it has 112,000. I would wait to clear the woods where there are deer. The farms are far off the road. You never see a dog. Of course, I would like to see that same OSP car coming my way, and ripping back, after me, the same sweet faced man who wishes he did not have to do this.

I wonder if I could enchant a rock. I to have no problem with humans. Bless my mother, my grandmother, and my genes. Oh well, dreams. Paul Simon has it right and speaks to my wanting to have it all.

The open palm of desire…Wants everything…It wants everything… It wants everything.

Dave can barely write his name anymore, let alone spell, but the rest of us played Scrabble when the kids were here, Patrick, Katie, and grandson Grant, who is ten. I was kibitzing, not having the patience to sit forever. These go on for hours. Grant is a dynamite player. His defensive game could make a strong woman weep.

At the end, each having no more than three or four tiles, Grant had a combo he wanted so badly, but could not have, lacking one letter. It just was not there. We were urging him to play his short word. He kept saying, "But I want this, I want to make this word." I was annoyed, wanting him to accept the reality, his parents, of course, more patient.

Now, a couple of weeks later, I see we are the same. I too have "the open palm of desire," have always. So why not for him?

MARCH 29, 2006

The juice of a good day suddenly lost its sugar when I hear of an old woman dying alone. No name mentioned. The fact she was Jewish has special import, but I would be saddened nonetheless. The news came from our Rabbi who wanted mourners for her service. I won't go, but will think of her.

Old people dying alone, tiny desiccated bodies, curled up in a fetal position, like my paternal grandmother when she died at 96. Tiny desiccated bodies in the camps. Dying without family. The ultimate horror.

I am determined to have my family with me when I die—I want to be able to tell them each some special memory, and how much I love them.

My mother chose to die alone. I can only guess she didn't want us to see her horrible wasting.

My little brother Jimmy was allowed to visit, stayed with her through it. He said her head looked like a skull. Why did he tell me that? He is fascinated by the base. Perhaps he is more honest than many of us.

One of the cats laid a chewed bird at the doorstep last night. I did check it out, curious about the process. It was dead after all, no more pain for it. Oddly relieved it was a sparrow, not one of the goldfinches. I hated it when our cat Jack caught goldfinches out of the air, so much like grabbing at popcorn jumping out of a topless pan. I feel badly that I prefer goldfinches to sparrows, though I like them too. If a cat got one of my doves, it would be nightmares for many nights—but then, they're not mine, are they?

We have a skull and some bones in the garden, brought in by the dogs from the pasture. Old dead sheep we have hauled out for the vultures, the coyotes, the bugs and flies. And what appears to be a deer skull. Curious indeed.

The other day while wandering the garden, Simone solemnly told me, "Some animals have died here." Some of her hens have disappeared, probably taken by hawks. She is learning about death. She told me she had not seen Roxy for a few days, speculated that she is dead.

No juice left tonight, but enough to help lay that poor woman to rest tomorrow, in my heart at least.

March 31, 2006

This morning we are working on mailings. Dave gets stuck every few minutes and cannot figure out what to do next, even though it is exactly the same thing he has been doing for the last few hours. I ask him what he sees when he looks at the work and is not sure what to do. He says "A lot of confusion, this here, that over there. Someone is doing something but I don't know what it is." I ask him who is doing it. He says, "I don't know, it is someone who knows how to do this." This strikes both of us as very funny, so we giggle.

He works better if things are kept orderly and there is not too much on the table. He has always been neat and kept his areas uncluttered. It was absolutely necessary when he had his own business, David N. Kent Company. They did insurance inspections, risk assessments, for companies in Los Angeles. There was a huge amount of detail involved. I was always amazed when he came home after seeing twenty different properties, usually apartments and commercial buildings, condo projects. His clipboard had one sheet for each "risk." All that was on the page was a few hen scratchings. He was able to remember, somehow, what it all meant.

He would get up at five the next morning to dictate full reports on forms he had designed himself. He had two file cabinets full of copies of his reports, filed perfectly alphabetically by streets, to be used in following years for "re-inspections." Often the property owner would change insurance companies. A new report request, not referencing the old, would be sent. He nearly always recognized the address and could refer to his original report. An incredible memory.

When we drove around town, he would point: "I did that building, this building, that market over there."

A year or so after our families began socializing, I was visiting his wife, Sherrill, and popped my head into Dave's office upstairs. He was at work dictating his reports and wearing glasses. I can still remember the little charge I got seeing him in such a different role from our social one. He looked so business-like.

Competency is high on my list of turn-ons. I admire it in women as much as men. It has a certain magnetic power. Or maybe it makes me feel safe. Thomas once accused me of attacking him when he was down. Perhaps I did. Somehow threatened. Maybe I was afraid he would not be able to take care of me, protect me. I liked seeing him at work in the courtroom. Maybe if I had gone more often our marriage would have held together, I would not have been trying to find what I did not have with him through other men.

The other men? It really was not about sex, rather, companionship, attention, reinforcement – and certainly excitement.

Dave thrills me when he plays his trumpet. I love it when he finishes a solo, lowers his horn, looks at me, smiles a secret smile, and winks. It is really no wonder I am still here.

April 2, 2006

This morning listening to Paul Williams, I was overcome with such longing - longing to experience again the feelings I did when I first heard his music. The ache was womb deep—I nearly turned it off.

It was part of the soundtrack of our courtship, especially during the many long evenings I spent at his apartment when we first started seeing each other. We fell in love in his bed as much as anywhere. Or at least I did. He protested for a couple of months that he was not sure what love is. And no wonder he was gun-shy, Sherrill leaving him for another man. Falling in love is so intoxicating I nearly lost my wits. Sometimes I would not return home until sunrise.

Our dear baby-sitter Paula, asleep on the couch, apparently worldly enough to be able to smile on us. She was a nurse in England during the war and lost her husband, an Earl, in those days. I can only imagine her take on how precious life, and love, is.

I was grabbing at life again. Those last years with Thomas were a horror. Ask the kids, they will tell you. They will tell you about the time we all came back from a dog show the night he returned from Dallas…arrived home before we did. He was so enraged we were not there to greet him. As soon as I walked in the door, he grabbed my purse, took all the credit cards, gave me twenty dollars and said, "Go, go so that I don't hit you."

I have read many times that you marry the same man over and over if you do not figure out what went wrong. I must have figured it out. Finding a powerful man who did not want to subjugate me, and the children, could have been tricky. Lucky for us, there was one right on our doorstep.

After we married, the children were among the first things we disagreed about. He felt entitled to discipline them. As he had been required to do with Sherrill's daughter, as my step-father had with us. That was quickly dead ended. *No one messes with my kids.* Dave accepted it with grace, did not want to do it anyway, just thought that was what fathers were supposed to do (as his authoritarian one.)

Control. Isn't that a (if not the) big issue in relationships? That fine dance of who gets to say how it will be. The tension between wanting what you want, and hoping the other will not have to give up too much, that he gets what he wants. As much as I love irony, this has gone a little far. Actually, I do love irony enough that I can chuckle at this. Though with ruefulness.

I have absolute control over everything now, except the most important thing: whom I'm now married to.

༄

Stop leaving me now
Perhaps tomorrow, next day.
I am not ready

Yet go if you must
Another day, tomorrow
Not now my lover

I am not ready
Please stay a little longer
Kiss me one more time

To my bed once more
Arms once more around my soul
Stay now my beloved.

༄

Chapter 24

APRIL 3, 2006

Time change, daylight savings (this is a silly name. For those of us who wake early, it is daylight lost.) My usual four o'clock wake up, became five o'clock, which is an okay wake up time, coffee brews at five-thirty, so I got up. All went well until about four pm, which was three old time, when I should have gotten my energy back.

I did have an energized conversation with Jen for an hour or so, then read a little bit of *Fabric of the Cosmos*.

I love thinking about what the universe is really about, how it is made, how it got here. It seems the closer science gets to understanding the origin, the more it parallels the account in the Kaballah. Before creation there was only *Ain Sof*. *Ain Sof* has no attributes, pure consciousness. *Ain Sof* had to withdraw a bit, pull aside in order to create a space or void for the universe to come into being. This sounds like making room for that pin-head sized Black Hole from which the universe exploded.

I also like to think what it means that light from earth is right now reaching systems many light years away. If 1943, my birth year, is just now getting somewhere, does that mean there is a part of the universe in which I am being born?

How fun to think about, is that a sort of Heaven? We are forever alive somewhere?

April 4, 2006

Bit of a tense day: two hours in the dentist chair, tension about a low tire, also having to stay within the speed limit and scold the Beemer for leading me astray. Then coming home to see Dave had put a bunch of stamps on the wrong side of the mailing.

I am gradually learning to leave that alone, not mention it, though this time I did again…he cannot help himself and my taking out my frustration on him only makes both of us feel bad.

I'm so relieved about a friend of mine who has had a couple of strokes. Today I learned they were attributed to a curable abscess so he will be okay.

His daughter Angelica was in my Hebrew School class when she was five. What a charmer and a beauty. Really, all of those little girls were: Dana, Sophie, Isabelle. And the little minx Olivia. Not really aware of their own perfection—just full of themselves in the most life affirming way. I considered it a big tribute to their parents.

I can clearly remember Angelica standing on her chair and confidently reading from her Hebrew primer. Dana telling perfectly the Exodus story; Sophie in the garden, leading us in meditation; Izzy crushed when we killed an earwig. (Her mother took me to task for that one, though I was not the person who squished it.) And Olivia, the girl with the dancing eyes, taking it all in. My little girls could do no wrong: Stand on a chair, the table, hey, why not? What an excellent way for me to re-create my childhood and add to the pleasure of theirs.

The boys, not so much. Well, you know, they are always poking at things. And, insist on wearing helmets. Actually, Cory and Jack were sweet—just not as present as the girls, who thought I was pretty special (ah hah, that must be it!).

Dave is enthusiastic about my involvement with the Havurah and really likes Rabbi David. For a couple of years we would have a big picnic out here for the whole school. They were a lot of fun, but even pre-diagnosis, I am not sure Dave knew what they were doing here—any party is fine with him. Mother gave him a wooden sign that still hangs by our front door: "Support the Two Party System, One Party a Week Is Not Enough."

April 5, 2006

Maybe it's just today, or yesterday, or last week, or last month. I am worried I am running out of emotion or out of caring. About the big things. Only those very close matter to me right now. And, even then, I lose patience. I love old Meggie, and will cry when we bury her, but her constant nearness, especially when she moves so slowly ahead of me, and the constant panting, is so trying. And Cindy, deaf and dominant, shrill bark to protect her territory, jolts me several times a day.

I am feeling so fragile. And angry. Angry that I have to pull back my emotions to protect others, Dave particularly. Just now, he (gently) pushed Kittyrings off his lap. I joked: "Why are you sending my cat away?"

He jumped. I said "I did not mean to scare you." He said, "It must have been about the argument today." I do not remember any argument, but he suggested things can get a little loud and rowdy when Simone is here. Or maybe he was thinking of yesterday when I was irritated he had put the stamps on the wrong side of the brochure. He thought that might have been it. I have asked him before if he is afraid of me. He has said not. It seems so. I must keep trying to anticipate how what I say and do affects him.

He does not know who Kathy is. This is so incredible to me I keep checking it. He knows she is an important person in our life, but not that she is our daughter. Today when she picked up Simone, he asked several times if she had a good trip. It seems that in his mind she is a traveling businesswoman whose child stays with us from time to time.

Now this is true. But why she would be here he doesn't seem to question. Kathy and I surmise it's because when she moved here from Seattle she dressed differently from what he remembered, business clothes, and did travel. He cannot tie her to the child he knew at three, or who lived in our house as a teen, our daughter. The trip to Santa Cruz to take her to college, the Junior High plays, her graduation…it's just not there.

Just now when I told him Jennifer was coming in ten days, I asked him if he knows who Jennifer is. He said, "Yes, your daughter." After double questioning, he remembers Patrick, and now Kathy, "The same situation, your children." I say, "Yes, our children." He: "Yes, but not out of me."

I have never explored with him his reason for not wanting his own children. No one could have been more present for mine than he.

It makes me a little dizzy sick when I recognize that part of our life, so important to me, has gone from his memory.

I have turned just now to look out on the pasture, the yards, to see the two remaining roosters jump up to the high branches, four rams having a conference, while one, Charlie, for reasons of his own, stands by the barn observing. The llamas are scattered and grazing, except for bratty Dempsey who is on the alert, neck up, just looking for a fight. What is with this guy?

Ok, there he goes, around the barn, challenging the castrati, Domino, all necks up now, everyone coming in. Rams oblivious, this is a llama situation, the *confrontation at high dusk*. Sukkot back to grazing for a moment, scratching his ear, probably a ploy. Here comes Domino, calling out Baby Dinosaur. Dempsey is out of my line of sight, but you can be sure he is the instigator... haven't seen Abraxis, the big Dad, never challenged. Necks still up on the two I can see. Must be happening on the creek. Ah yes, walking that way, now with heads lowered. Oh, there is Abraxis, looking mighty. What a good guy, the powerful one, the only one who is secure enough to let me touch him.

Hmm, apparently it was a before-bed feint, they are in mid-macho trance. It is over. Other than a couple of ripped ears in the adolescent days, no one gets hurt.

Oh we do so love it here.

Again and again the mantra: *I want to be alone here.* I do not want to stop, step around animals, getting up over and over to check on Dave I have no flow. And the near constant worry for them.

Yesterday going to town to the dentist, I was full of foreboding, was so relieved to drive up to the house with body and car intact, but still worried. I was so relieved to see the dogs come out to greet me, thinking one of them may have died while I was gone the mere four hours. I guessed it must therefore be Dave who had dropped.

Was I relieved he hadn't? Not really. I want this to be over. Throw me in the pit for that thought? I do not know. Probably not.

April 6, 2006

I felt so very good all day. Last night's entry really did something, catharsis, I feel more relaxed today. My patience is no longer patience, just being in the situation, no force, let it go. I know this will change from day to day, the anger, sometimes rage, will continue to come out. The patience I have for Simone is the model. She is four, after all. But so is he.

Acknowledging to myself his death might be a relief, is just a human thing, but wants to be hidden under my guise of goodness.

I have all it takes to reach for *Good*, but wanting for myself will not stop me or others, from loving me.

Chapter 25

APRIL 7, 2006

I suppose it is a good thing, keeps me emotionally honest, this intense mind-body connection. But sometimes, I'd just as leave do without.

This morning I awoke so tired, I could not have left the house if a fire broke out. And I knew exactly what it was. Errands. Kathy and I were to stop at the airport where I had to sign for a ticket I was giving to Roxy on my frequent flyer miles.

Then on to Lowe's to buy a fridge (our old one leaks) and to sign a contract for the flooring. Maybe downtown to pay my speeding ticket. Does any of this sound like fun to me? With a good book waiting and wanting to play with the Newsletter? My body didn't think so.

Well, mind and body compromised. Airport only (deadline is tomorrow to secure the reservation). Roxy's being away for three months is a gift to us all right now, except perhaps for Simone. Of course, as usual, once underway, I was more or less normal energy. Though the hour back and forth seemed interminable.

It is hard for me to commit to anything anymore; I always get sick. Signing up for the Women's *Seder* is a gamble. Last year two days before Anne's *Seder*, to which I was bringing lots of food and was supposed to help, I got the flu. I missed Emily's, Danielle's and Yuval's B'nei Mitzvahs. And who knows what ever else more?

Once back home, not only was I on track, but also motivated Dave to mow the lawn (first of the season and a mega challenge) while I trimmed with the weed eater. The garden has been driving me nuts with the tall wet grass and overbearing weeds.

I feel like I'm at war with myself. My body telling my mind: I am in charge, don't you tell me what to do! My emotions caught somewhere in the middle. *Oh laws.* Maybe this is a rebellion against the "perfect child" me. The one who could recite *The Night Before Christmas* at three-years-old (I seriously doubt that story) and insisted on matching my clothes at four (plausible).

I want what I want when I want it. I am a child. Dressed up in grownup clothes and obligations.

I like it that people like me, and feel guilty when I am not with them if that is what they want. Friends calling, wanting to talk, get together, but I bury myself, in myself. Maybe if I get a couple of years when no one notices I am gone…nah, wouldn't like that.

It is ironic that I help create creatures to love me. And am there for them, but so much less so for humans. Oh, probably not, I want creatures to love, not to love me. That sounds like what it is really about.

This book I am reading *Our Inner Ape*, tells of the emphatic nature of our closest relative, the bonobos. I am looking for clues everywhere – clues to life, clues to *my* life.

I know one thing, if I don't get back to gardening soon, I'll go bonkers. Nah, just want to do it. The cozy winter indoors has overstayed its welcome.

April 8, 2006

Finished *Our Inner Ape* today. Another kick back lazy Shabbat, so nice and needed. It is a vindication of sorts for me, sometimes embarrassed by my emotionalism. A reason why I cry at weddings of strangers, or even fictitious ones on the screen.

The author, with extraordinary documentation from decades working with primates, posits that our capacity for empathy, our moral ground, our ability to have stable communities is tied to our evolution. That morals come not from the top down, e.g. religions, political constructions, enlightened leaders, but are seated in our early genetic development and share much with our closest relatives the bonobos and the chimps.

It is an enlightenment for me. Why the Ten Commandments, and many of the 613, seem so obvious. All this time I thought it is because I am a Jew. Well, both the chimps and the bonobos have their own groups where different rules apply. So, hey, I am firmly linked in this evolutionary chain.

There is this one amazing observation. A bonobo female sees a bird that has fallen. She tries to revive it by lifting its wings, jiggling it a little. When that doesn't work, she climbs a tree, opens its wings and sails it off. She knows how to save the bird. It did not fly then, but landed unharmed to fly a few hours later. This is so extraordinary: empathy *among* animal species.

What a relief, I am one of the good guys. Well, did not really doubt it, I feel like a good guy, life affirming.

Tense moment this morning when a spider walked in from outside as Meggie was coming in the same door. Confuse Meggie by making sure she does not step on the spider, or risk the spider? I closed my eyes and hoped for the best. This time it worked. The spider scuttled under the dishwasher.

I am not particularly extreme in my love of animals. Empathy is the ability to know, or guess, what the other creature is experiencing. But how can one do that unless she has the same memory bank of experience, a link on the same chain of life?

April 9, 2006

... the exclusive Point Hamiltair area of Lake Arrowhead in ...

I just googled this after having talked to my cousin Dawn, our reminiscences about Arrowhead...It made me queasy. Sad, teary. Someone has taken our Hamiltair. The eighty acres that Grandpa Hamilton had for us. His family. A huge clan radiating affection and sharing fun and laughter.

We spent every summer there. Walking up from the Boathouse bare-footed on the gravel. To the Daughters' House. Sometimes from the Daughters' House to the Gate Lodge and back. A little scary, we had heard stories of bears.

When we were older, and no longer afraid of bears, we would get up at dawn and meet at the dock for the pristine hour of water skiing. No one else was on the lake. The water was a mirror. Truly a mirror. With her father, my Uncle Harold, driving the Chris Craft, we skied double.

I think now how athletic we must have been, to rise out of the water together, each on one ski. We never tried as a double the step off the dock, though each of us could do it individually.

Oh yes! Schussing back and forth, big rooster tails. Pure joy. Of course, we never fell. Why would we? The perfect mind-body connection. One of those perfect states of freedom tempered by control.

I want to soar like that again. Fly.

Chapter 26

APRIL 11, 2006

This morning Dave was looking out on the pastures and said, "Home, home on the range." He talked about what a nice home we live in and that, "People come here and socialize and say whatever they feel like saying." I don't know what he meant by that. Maybe he had Kathy and Simone in mind. They live so close that they visit many hours a week.

Today I had three goals: finish our tax return, work on the newsletter, and go to Rainey's for provisions. Finished the taxes this morning, and just now did all I could with the NL until more people send in their submissions. Will go to Rainey's in a bit. I love having projects and seeing them to completion. A lot of satisfaction in the process and the product. I hate housecleaning – in part because it is never finished.

My mother kept a perfect house. Everything always in order, not a spec of dust. It was a pleasant environment to live in, but had its drawbacks. We all had to get up together on weekends – no sleeping in – because she wanted to fix breakfast and clean up. It seemed out of order to her for us to fix our own meals at any old time.

It used to bother me when she would get up from the table as soon as dinner was finished to do the dishes. She was so compulsive about this that it took years to train her that at our house, we left the dishes until the morning. Why spoil the comfortable social after dinner time? My stepmother was the same way. She and I got into a huge fight one night because I wanted to stay at the table to chat with Daddy rather than help her in the kitchen. It was not a matter of not wanting to help – but what's the rush?

I am from a family of controlling women. Because I am that way myself, I understood their need to have things just the way they wanted it. For the most part, the men went along with this arrangement. They had their own areas of control.

It was a surprise to me when Dave and I first married he thought he was entitled to some say about where things went in the kitchen or were arranged in the house. Probably because he lived as a bachelor until he and Sherrill married when he was 33, and then again the several years after they divorced.

It was a bone of contention for him the only furniture (or really, any household stuff) I allowed him to bring with him was a little three drawer chest we put in the kitchen for tools, and four TV trays. Poor baby. But really… a recliner?

Maybe that is why I shattered under Thomas' rule. One day he up and sold our little VW convertible (bright tomato red) and came home with a yucky big used American station wagon. Well, fortunately it had a front-end problem so, the next day, we traded it in for a new VW bus (at a loss on the wagon of a couple of grand in one day). What a jerk. Why didn't he ask me what I wanted?

Even if the writing was on the wall then, I would not have known how to go it alone. I thought by getting married so young I was making a choice for independence by escaping my controlling family. Even in Sausalito, with few friends and isolated from any family support system, it seemed as though it had been a good decision. The early sixties for people like me and the two friends I made there were no different from the fifties. Mom is the little wife, Dad the power and the provider. The provider part is good. Only years later did I realize I had made a mistake and missed socially participating in one of the most energizing decades of my lifetime.

My step-father tried to warn me. The evening Thomas and I told my parents of our plans, he beckoned me into the quiet of the pantry and said, "I think you are making a mistake." I said, "I know what I am doing." Hah, the arrogance of eighteen year olds. I became pregnant with Kathy a few weeks after our engagement, so the marriage was a given. Of course, that's a trade I would never take back.

April 12, 2006

Not only did the women of my family keep control of the daily life and environment, but also of the family secrets.

When my mother went off to the hospital for ten days for the birth of my sister Barbie, my father was never home. Maybe occasionally.

It was not for many years, when I was an adult I was told by mother she found out Daddy was in love with my Aunt Rosabelle. Apparently he could not make up his mind which woman he wanted, or to which situation he felt obligated, but he and mother stayed together for enough time to conceive Barbie. As usual, I blame my mother. But I did not know their story.

After the ten days, mother came home in an ambulance and was carried upstairs on a stretcher. I now think that was the most peculiar thing. Her birth had been easy. Barbie's birth was so imminent that on Mother's arrival at the hospital they tied her legs together to prevent the birth until the delivery room. These days she would be up and walking in a few hours.

Although I soon took her as my own, at first I was skeptical of the baby, why did we need her? I had my baby sister Kathy, and my little brother Chip. Plus, she was all red and peely and cried a lot.

I was six— knew nothing, was told nothing, *children seen, not heard.* Then this funny smelling nurse, Miss Lillian, came into our home to take care of Barbie, and Kathy also I suppose, as she was only two.

Mother fired her a year later because she allowed Barbie to play with her food, her peas. *Oh laws.* Not to mention Kathy swallowed a bottle of baby aspirin and had to be rushed to the hospital. Not to mention I threw tooth powder in Chip's eyes and he had to be rushed to the hospital.

Who were these people who seemed so often absent?

Next thing I knew, they told me they were divorcing. I must have known what it meant, or the grievousness was apparent, because I felt struck. I clearly remember the scene: We were in the dining room; I was standing next to Daddy who was sitting to my left in the big chair at the end of the table, that beautiful mahogany table with the stately carved chairs, burgundy fabric, Mother to the right of me, also sitting.

Soon after, Daddy moved out, and I moved to the hospital for ten days. Serious nephritis. Does my body know how to protect my emotions, or what? Well, I survived, unlike the little boy who had come in the day before me.

So the next thing, after having recovered at Grandma and Grandpa Montgomery's home. (What, you say, not with your parents? Well is not this story telling its own tale?), we spent some time with Daddy and Aunt Rosabelle. She said, "Don't call me Aunt Rosabelle, I am not your aunt any more." She had been the wife of my mother's brother, Uncle Tommy. I can remember thinking what a coincidence it was that she and Uncle Tommy were also getting a divorce. Hah.

This was our first vacation together as a second family beach house in Hermosa. We all loved the ocean. And of course, also there were my cousins, Roxanne and Tommy, soon to become my step-sister and brother. *Oh laws.*

The most amazing thing: they did not sleep together. Somehow, in my child mind, this did not make sense. At seven years old, I knew nothing about sex, but I knew the 'mom' and the 'dad' slept together. Much later I learned they did not, at her insistence, have sex before they were married. What a confusing time it was for us children.

Time for Johnny Cash and *Walk the Line*, sure my life will seem simple after listening to his.

A little while later I am listening to Dylan, *Thunder Mountain*, to just shake loose, get up and dance. Dave peeked around the corner. I pulled him in to dance. We do the Texas Two step and Swing like the crazy people we are. And he, the jazz musician he is, chimed in with jive talk, "Hey lady, ain't I seen you 'round here, you pretty girl." And I, "Well, I jus' drop by to see how you dance."

We still have fun. The basic heart, the core of what makes us move, has not changed.

April 13, 2006

I wonder how necessary it is to recognize my mortality. It is supposed (according to whom?) to be one of the growing up, or aging, things that we do. A show I liked a decade or so ago, *Fame*, had the most wonderful song, which I am in the process of downloading now: *I'm going to live forever*. Hey, I buy it. Well, the download is taking a long time on the phone line, so, let's put on Bo Diddly instead. Just the thing! In the moment! In every moment! Ah, we all know this, but when we actually do it, it is clear. *We are living forever* – in our intense one on one encounters, face to face, or on the phone, or against a sheep who wants to go this way while you want it to go that, or with that clump of grass you'll sacrifice your back to dig out – *I am here, alive*.

Today, Dave reveled in the views. "How beautiful this house is, the views." He loves the long view, always has. I am rather partial myself to the long view in nature, the short view in life.

Oh good Jiminy, here comes now again Etta with "*I would rather go blind boy, then see you walk away, see you walk away, from me.*" The thing about the Blues is it speaks to the angst, but does it in such a chipper way a lot of the time. Life can feel like left-over garbage, but, hey, that is just the way it is. Or not. Now listening to another, there is not so much chipper. Blues is Blues. That's probably why they call it that.

I don't get why I am so attached to the Blues. My life is nothing like that. Any man done me wrong, I'd just get shet of him, one way or another.

This morning very early I heard the rooster's warning yells, never mistaken for their crowing. Ran out to barn two where it was coming from. Yes indeed, four young coyotes. Oh aren't they just the thing? Probably one of natures perfect creations… not just beautiful, but true survivors. (Along with rats, cute also, and flies and roaches, not so cute, though interesting). I was relieved the roosters had not been attacked (yet), but gently urged the yotes to go off, gently only, so they would not leave so quickly I could not have a good look at them. I take videos of all of this in my head. Joy to me on my deathbed. Wait, hello, what deathbed?

April 14, 2006

This morning he was wandering around so I asked him if he felt alright. He said, "Yes, a little disoriented is all…." I asked him if something was bothering him. He said, "No, I'm very happy, all these new people coming in here, the work we do." It reminded me I had forgotten to tell him Beth is coming for lunch tomorrow. He said, "Oh good, it's been some time since we've seen her." *Yes, three weeks, maybe a month.* He: "Oh is that all?" I: "Well, I think so but time goes so fast these days I'm not sure."

A minute or two later, he said, "You know, I didn't like Beth when I first met her." I was surprised, had not heard that, so said, "Yes, well she can be very direct sometimes." He: "Yes, I like that now, but was feeling protective of you."

Now, that is a whole conversation he participated in with nary a glitch, a rare occurrence. My protector, now the protected.

I will be so glad to see her. Though I have other confidants, including my daughters, there are many things we share I would not tell my girls. It is not as though they would not understand. It just feels squirrelly. I told her we would be having Boeuf Bourgeon, a favorite of both of us, and Kathy who will of course join us. (Bless her heart, she did the shopping.)This will be a test for me. It is Pesach week, no leavened foods. I had Kathy buy a baguette, necessary for my traditional (almost said rigid) menu. To eat or not to eat? Beth said "Just throw it on the floor, stomp on it, and call it unleavened.

I know I am somewhere on the upswing of the Bell Curve of intelligence, but I am a genius when it comes to picking friends. Wait, hello, they are picking you too. Okay, so they are geniuses also. What am I modest?

There was that really funny moment at our 25th anniversary, the time for tributes to the wonderfulness of Dave and me and our togetherness. Our nephew Jeffery saying the sweetest things, one of which being, "Aunt Michelle is so modest." His mother, darling Courtney, followed with sweet tributes, started with: "I have never known Aunt Michelle to be modest." She did not mean it for the laugh, which came, and Jeff chagrined (that was worked out). They both were right, I suppose. Maybe he meant humility. Me and

Moses, the most humble man on earth. And why not, he saw the face of God.

It is all that free will and determinism stuff again. Knowing you are clueless, but go marching on, following all the millions of directions from your firing neurons. Which includes path choices. I think of Dorothy and the boys, selecting their path. The shriveling feet of the Wicked Witch of the East, and the melting Wicked Witch of the West (oh, the wonderful Margaret Hamilton) are my favorite scenes from *The Wizard of Oz*. Well, I am also partial to the flying monkeys. Oh, forget it, nothing I do not like.

Dorothy, the Tin Man and the Scarecrow are walking down the Yellow Brick road, scared out of their wits. They have chosen this path. We, the audience have no doubt of their success. The omniscience of the audience. We do have a bit of that, being the audience of our own lives. Lions and tigers and bears, oh my. But the lion, a pretty easy going one: it could be out there. The frightening "out there." Or not. Sometimes I just go with the flow. I cannot control it all.

My Hebrew name: Michal Rut Bot Yisrael. Michal: who is like God. What does that mean? A gift or a curse?

Chapter 27

April 14, 2006

There is a certain freedom in not being able to define the perfect life.

Revisiting this:

There was a man once.

The last time I dared leave Dave to go to New York. Sukkot with Jen and the boys. After apple picking, we went to a children's museum. I was sitting on a bench while the boys were working on the train system.

I looked up across the room. There was a man there I knew I could have been with in a different life. We would have gone to the Met and the opening shows.

I wrote all about it on my cocktail napkin on the way home on the plane. Saved it, but after a couple of months, tore it up, would not have wanted Dave to see it.

When I walked out into the garden this morning, I was going especially to check on the two forsythias I planted last spring, placing them just so. Their bright yellow will be one of the first colors to show at the close of winter – one in the south-west corner, the other in the north section, next to the virgin's bower. They are not impressive yet... but *next year*. It is always *next year* for gardeners. This is a garden started more than twenty years ago and not yet complete.

The *next years* are becoming fewer. As I see Dave sliding toward eighty and losing his mind in the process it becomes harder to believe there will ever be *the* perfect garden. Well I suppose we were never meant to return to Eden.

April 16, 2006

I am frustrated, angry. I would have liked to have been at the Women's *Seder* tonight. Beth and I have a special connection, but it makes me crazy that she calls up and just arrives. My energy and attention is so thin these days. One extra surprise is almost more than I can bear.

The newsletter takes such focus; this month's mailings are here to do also. For a few hours some of my attention was taken by attending Simone's Easter egg hunt, and in the back of my mind the details for the casserole to prepare for the Seder.

Then Beth calls: "Since you are not available on Sunday, may I come Saturday?" So Friday, I cooked the Bourguignon she relishes, and made preparations for the rest of the meal. And on Saturday, Shabbat for crying out loud, I checked linens and silver, dusted, vacuumed, made the beds and cleaned the bathrooms because she notices. Well, all might have been okay, but at the beautiful table I had set, the perfect meal, with Kathy, Simone, and Beth's grandson, Jack, she and I got into an argument over CEO compensation. *What are you so angry about, who cares?* She won't tap into it. Tap into why she is so angry. I just was not in the mood, stretched so thin. Though I always rise to the bait. Kathy attempted to enter the conversation, "Maybe you two should go into the other room for a hug." Beth: "No, we like it this way." Well, I usually do, but don't like arguments when the opposition has no ground, no documentation.

Then, this morning, as they are my guests, I provided breakfast, served with only a little resentment but with the knowledge I was sapping my energy for the cooking still to be done, not to mention the energy for the Seder itself.

I did make the casserole, supposed to be for twelve...turned out to be for twenty. And was interrupted regularly by Dave's imploring for this or that. He should be my first consideration, my social life is secondary. So the wonderful rice, cheese, chili, broccoli casseroles are in the refrigerator. And I am home, not at the Seder, too exhausted by the last days. Darn it anyway.

Well, at least we will have food for many days.

Just went out to check on Dave. The TV was off. I thought he had gone to bed, though it is not yet seven. He is out raking the deck. Yea! This guy wants to be present, and loves the outdoors. The deal is, I do not want anyone expecting anything from me. Go away. Go away. I am content here. I want only my husband, my children, and grandchildren. And one or two friends on *my terms*. Do not march into my space. My guys, Peter, the UPS man, Bruce, our mechanic, Ron, our dead-car-taker-awayer, dear Dale Schultz, our alfalfa man, Mike and Bobby Rainey, up at the corner store. These are the people in my life.

It might be just as well I didn't make it to the Seder I would have been in outer space, my face saying what was expected, my head nodding appropriately, absorbing the face of she who is talking, but hearing no words, just taking in the face. My sisters.

Many days, all I want is peace. One day I will be dragged out of here in a wagon. Two horses will pull it, matched bays. Clopping along just so, with their own purpose. I will be in the box. No one has figured out how to transport me in a shroud without damage to the skin. We who are still living forget damage to the skin is of no import to a dead person. At the end of the driveway, there will be another mode of transportation, a hearse I suppose. To take me to the cemetery. The horses could not trot that far. And the entourage will either be too bored, or to engaged in their own thoughts to remember the occasion. Well why not, they are still alive.

April 17, 2006

This diary is riddled with my pre-occupation with death. I was twelve the first time I saw a dead person. He was Grandma's friend. I was visiting her in Milwaukee. She went to the viewing, as was the custom, and took me along. I do not think she particularly wanted me to be there, but could not leave me at home alone. She was the only person in my childhood whom I trusted completely. It was a long room with grey, soft, carpet. We walked up to the casket. No one else was there. Grandma held my hand. There was this old man, frozen, and smelling peculiarly sweet. I would recognize that smell if I ever experienced it again. It comes back to me when I think of death. The box he was in was as high as my neck. It was heavy and black. And there was a dead person in it. I am sure I had no idea what it all meant and find it odd that I still remember the scene so clearly.

It wasn't until I was seventeen that I saw another dead person. My Grandfather Montgomery. Mother and I went to the funeral home together. He was in a little room, candles and such, grayness around. He looked waxen, shrunken, his face was different. They had put his arms somehow so you could see the watch he had always worn. Mother and I sat there for a while. He had loved my mother. A woman came in, someone my mother knew a long time ago. They greeted each other. But moments before that, the woman had looked in and said, "I must be in the wrong room, that is not Vic." He sure didn't look like the grandfather I had known for seventeen years, the robust smiling man who had a special fondness for me, his first grandchild. He called me Mickey.

Today when Simone and I were playing cards, *Crazy Eights*, and *Go Fish*, I told her about how her great-great Grandfather had taught me to play cards. In their library, filled bookshelves were on every wall except the wall with the window above window seats that overlooked the rolling lawn of the front yard. That's where the game table was. We played solitaire, double of course. The regular kind and many variations.

I told her also about being back in the potting shed, where he taught me how to transplant chrysanthemums. No dead smell there. Just the soil. He showed me how to crack the clay pot just so, not disturbing the roots. Then how to move it on to the larger pot, more room, more soil, bring it to its flowering.

I am very sad. All these good people go away. And one of the best, my husband, is walking slowly out that door. I wonder if I will still be here when he leaves for good.

༄

Sun setting on a dream
May rise in one other perfect guise
A child's face and heart

༄

Chapter 28

APRIL 18, 2006

Well that was trippy. Jennifer blowing in here like an electric storm.

The boys so grown in just six months, their smiles, real smiles, happy to see me. Walked out and around, re-explored the tree house, too small for them now. Back in to the familiar Legos. Just comfortable here. We are together only about fourteen or so days a year. They know their roots when they see them.

The joy of my girls Jen and Kathy and I, just jabbering on. So much to say, so much to see in each others face, telling the stuff we cannot convey on the phone, though the outlines are there. The shy laughing about the possibility of new loves, new hopes. Oh, did I see you blushing? Well, just a little. Oh I love my girls. I am one of them, it is the *us*.

APRIL 21, 2006

When I was in the shower just now, getting ready for Shabbat dinner, I tried to let the hot water relax me. I leaned my forehead on my hands against the wall, hot water pounding my back to relieve the sciatic pain that has been bad the last couple of days. I noticed, again, I am plagued with shoulds, oughts, and calendars. Calendars with squares marking out every day, certainly, but also every hour. *Before the girls come back from the Science Museum with the* kids, I have to vacuum, print mailing labels for Dave to work on the mailings, and try a diary entry.

This was the first time I had seen how I box myself in — into those squares that try to corral time.

It reminded me of when I was four and going to Miss Buckley's school in Los Angeles. The playground had the usual swings and such, and was surrounded by a chain link fence.

What I remember about that yard was my having to stand in a square in a line with the other kids. I do not remember what we did in that square, why we were there, just that I hated it. I have no memories of playing.

I suppose that is why I was so permissive with my own kids. There were few rules: be kind, do not put yourself in mortal danger, and do not limit your life choices (You ARE going to get good grades because you ARE going to college.)

I just did what I felt was right. Seemed to work. A big bit of that outcome is bounding through our life right now. Those boys of hers, Jennifer's mothering, an amazement. Open, active, curious, sweet, funny, gooney, super smart, and at last, the twins, Erez and Natan, at nine years old, some self-control.

It has been a long road. Each of the twins has some neurochemical imbalance. Meds have helped tremendously. But the parenting of Jen and Andrew (even though now apart) the love and the constancy, has been the anchor for these amazing kids.

And I am repaid over and over as a participant, a real participant in my children's lives. Though probably less than I imagine. Sometimes I will say something and Jen and Kathy will look at each other with a little grin and flash of eyes, their secret, that I do not know.

It is okay. Their loving each other is gift enough.

April 22, 23, 2006

"Seems to me birds are getting pretty tame to people." This was Simone's comment when I tried to track down the details of the serious burial of the red finch.

Well, I knew most of it, just could not remember which child had held the bird to his chest last night to feel its heart beating.

They were engaged in a Rug Rat movie, the response was slow. Five-year-old Ari, Jennifer's youngest, piped up and said, "Oh that was me."

We have many bird feeders. Occasionally a bird will crash into the window. Most fly off; often one is stunned and drops for a while. Or, more rarely, forever. This one was a bright rosy finch, huddled against the planter out in the yard beyond the kitchen. It seemed to be one of the surviving ones. Alas, wasn't to be, but not before the children could look at it, touch and hold it with compassion.

This morning I found it down dead. Ari discovered it. I suggested we bury it. The troops mobilized. Dug a hole, buried it, Erez found a big rock...asked for a marker to write on the stone. Long discussion by all participants as to what should be written. They wanted a name. "Red Finch" was the name agreed on. Simone wanted: "Red Finch, Dead Finch." "Rest in Peace" was unanimous.

The final marking on the tombstone: "Here lies Mr. Red Finch, The Dead Finch, R.I.P. They then went out to gather flowers. Even this morning the flowers were crisp. Tonight, they are also very dead.

A sparrow was found not too much later, stunned with a little bloody beak. *What is going on?* We put him up into the feeder, away from...whatever. Before I went to bed it was still there in the chill so I put a cover over it. This morning it was gone! Flown away! What a good thing to bring to these sleepy-headed kids who had spent the night.

Ah, the spending the night. The mothers, Kathy and Jennifer wanted to go to Ashland to have some town time with their cousins,

Heidi and Courtney. Lots of checking in. Making sure I was okay, the kids were okay. I just chuckled, told them the stories. "Have I not taken care of kids before?" Really, they are more worried about me. They think I am old. Hah!

Before the burial, Ari, Natan, and Simone played lion on the lawn then went to the barn to do a musical on the hay stack while Erez stayed in the yard, intent on digging the trench for our new pipeline. I tracked them with my video cam until I realized it was out of tape.

Well, that was okay. I have always been suspect of filming rather than experiencing. But still, I cannot claim it all in my memory. The films bring it back, nearly all.

Later Natan spent time at the computer to calm, center himself. Erez was still digging, driving to his goal of a complete trench. Then they again noticed the last light, the golden light, which they had already frisked through…through the tall seeding grasses.

"Grandma, let's go out to the pasture and see the llamas." What a precious little troop gathered near to me, very close as the llamas approached, serious, nervous, attentive (llamas: *What the heck is this coming at us?)* Nostrils flared, eyes wide, advancing, curiosity overtaking fear. A quick truce. Hey, *it is just llamas; hey, it is just the kids of the Two Legs.*

And then on to the sheep bones in the pasture graveyard. Old dog Cindy got lots of praise for leading the way to the bones.

Who is more fascinated by death than those who will not die? Death is not particularly fascinating to me anymore. That is probably a good thing for my kids. Bury the bird; look at the rib cage of a once alive sheep…What I am fascinated by is these new lives. So, so, present. "Grandma, Grandma, come here, quick, hurry, look at this: Have you ever seen such a big worm?"

In truth, I hadn't.

Chapter 29

APRIL 24, 2006

I am suddenly depressed on the most beautiful day of the year. I was weeding and trying to work hard soil that should have been friable after years and years of composting. The reality of the garden and the parallel to our life sometimes drops me to the ground which absorbs my tears. Facing my responsibility for continual feeding, nurturing, enriching made me a little queasy.

As much as I try to meet the challenge of the garden myself, I miss Dave's help. He had such strength, enough to bring in ten loads of barn scrapings to mulch the beds. He still sometimes says, "I can bring one more load." My man, always trying to please. His "one more load" now is so many fewer than five years ago.

As he physically deteriorates, so do I – I also am aging. So, always the fear, the question: *Will we one day have to leave?*

Next life I will require my body to keep up with what *I* want to do.

April 25, 2006

Everything is coming alive again after a blissfully long winter then a sudden spring.

Spent the morning, or a lot of it, scrunched down vacuuming, then washing, then prime coating the baseboards in the hall. Inspired, nice to have clean. But my body said a most emphatic "no" to moving on to the bathroom. Rats. Still two rooms to go after that.

Dave watched the news, oblivious to my puttering around. Such a sweet face when I explain what is happening—nodding and accepting. It sometimes makes me weak with sadness how compliant he is—no questions of "What the Hell is happening to me? I don't know what you mean, what you are saying."

His acceptance is right for him—no betrayal of his core being, his way of being in the world.

For me? I want to tell him everything about what is happening and reassure him I am following him, carrying him, through the dark tunnel to come. Perhaps my dark tunnel, not his.

My tunnel is not yet dark. I keep the lights shining with my memories, retreating into them more and more. I thought today if I were cast into outer space, floating, I would have nothing but my memories – they would keep me busy for a long time, thought not eternity, probably.

What would I miss, lack? I would miss a pen and paper to write it down.

April 26, 2006

Hello real world, crashing down again. The diversions were wonderful: almost a week of Jennifer and the kids, completely absorbing. In the twixt, finishing the Newsletter, starting on this month's mailings. The guys, Leroy and Brandon, Leroy with several rings in his ear and a stud in his tongue, putting in the kitchen floor.

A great moment when this was all happening at once: Dave at the end of the table with the mailings, the workers in the kitchen, the boys with their Legos behind Dave on the floor, the men with the most awful music (Jen informed me: heavy metal) blasting.

Dave looked up from his work and said, "This is really something." And it was.

Yesterday, I worked too hard toward the pre-carpet prep. Big crash. Body done for. Today, okay, accept, read, just lie on the couch and read, mellow with Simone, Gram's Day! Dave spent hour at the table, doing his favorite thing, the marketing mailings for Sandy, our only source of income.

But all of a sudden he lost it, and I freaked. Bigger 'lost it' than usual. He kept pointing to the brochure and said, "It's the same address, it is all going to the same address." He was distressed thinking we would lose business if one person got 1700 brochures. I kept showing him the address labels, trying to make him understand each piece went to a different address. Finally, oh, and what a relief, I realized he was referring to Sandy's return address, thinking that was where they were all going. Not good, but his misperception was comprehensible.

He became stressed again this afternoon when I suggested he mow a little more of the lawn, as he mentioned this morning. Around ten I reminded him: "No I want to wait until it is dryer." Three O' Clock: "No, it is too late."

So, I took it out on him around six: "You are still wearing your bathrobe. Please get dressed in the mornings, I am not living in a hospital ward." Next thing I know he is in the bathroom preparing to take a shower. So I sigh and extract him.

This is my deal, I claim it. *Do not cry for me Argentina*, I can cry for myself, though don't much, too much good stuff balances the sad, the scary.

And these kids of mine, so caring. They have organized a plan to all be here when Jen comes again this summer, including my sister's family; they will send us away and fix up and decorate the house. The girls started a bit this week coming home with a bright and happy bedspread and new sheets for our room.

The twins are still busy with their contribution: digging the trench for a permanent pipe to replace the garden hose that has been our source of water for four years—what relaxed country bumpkins we have been all this time.

And weaving in and out, the Princess Simone; the back drop to it all: the tree peonies ready to bloom, the most magical of flowers; the viburnum already with their pink white blossoms that smell like deepest passionate love.

April 27, 2006

Dave had a bit of a rough start this morning. He couldn't grasp collecting the wastebaskets from each room to take out to the trash can for the usual Thursday pickup. Moving the records, the old LPs, out to the garage eluded him also—he put them in his office instead. He was able, however, to get off a few good one liners and initiate our usual shtick morning play. And to put on some mailing labels, though slowly. Some lawn mowing went okay also for a bit, but then bogged down because he could not remember I had suggested we use the weed eater on the tall grass before he tries to go through it with the mower.

As at all his earlier downturns, I realize that nothing is settled beyond various contingencies and suddenly feel the intense urge to make plans. Right now it is important to me to get the painting done and the carpet laid. To get rid of clutter. I need a simple, happy, aesthetic environment to calm me and let me organize my life so I can take over what he no longer can do.

He is physically capable of doing almost as much as he was five years ago; the problem is he cannot think things through. Halfway through emptying the dishwasher he starts loading in dirties. He cannot grasp the sense of things, the reason and order. And then, of course, cannot remember when I tell him.

Washing laundry used to be one of his favorite chores, but since the bleach incident, bleach instead of detergent, and the fact he pours the detergent directly on the dry clothes, laundry is off limits to him now.

If I do not create plenty of time, relaxed time, time not allotted to my own work and pleasure, things get tense. I read that multi-tasking makes you stupid – it is worse than that for me – it makes me angry and impatient. His not being able to drive now is another household handicap.

As is his difficulties with envisioning future events with any accuracy. Today we were moving the stereo equipment. He wanted to put it on the deck, I said, "No, it might get rained on." Well it is a magnificent sunny day, so in his world, what is now, is always. So he: "It's not going to rain."

But on the other side, if I mention a future event which involves us both, kids coming, doctor appointment, it nags at him. I made the mistake of telling him his cousin Judy had e-mailed. For hours he was concerned he might have to call her.

His old band leader from Dixieland days, Larry Barnard, called wanting to bring over a video of the band. I didn't even tell him. I did not call Larry back. He would like to see the video, but not to have to try to remember. Nostalgia is not part of his world now. What a pity.

A couple of months ago he was willing talk on the phone to our adorable Tommy Stamper, the drummer in his band, a favorite of us both. And got it right for the most part but he might not have known who he was talking to during the whole conversation. What a bummer. Better he were on his death bed with awareness, to hear of their love. This is a sinking.

Funny, he remembers Jennifer as his daughter, Patrick as his son, but not Kathy right now. The girls surmise he is tapping into the old memories for them, but Kathy is so much part of this recent life that he puts her in a different place, as though a new person has wiped out the old. She seems okay with it, but it distresses me.

Oh, jeeze, he is out in the kitchen making slamming noises, have to go.

Also, we have *Brokeback Mountain* on DVD.

April 27, 2006, Addendum

I just got back from Rainey's and had to put it down (but not before segueing into the garden to smell the viburnum and lilacs, which last only for a blink).

I went for candy for Dave, chicken feed, cigarettes, gas and air in a tire. And, to get out of the house. To my social refuge where I bury myself in country. My body language changes, my voice, vocabulary. A particular home. My no makeup, tee shirt and jeans, graying hair in a pony tail, my weathered 60ish look. A good old boy flashes me a look, and comes to open the door, which I have capably already opened myself.

Says he: "Let me give you a hand." Says I, with a glint, "I though you might." Ever the flirt. Though as Kathy said, "But such a nice one, you make them feel good about themselves." And why not?

I had to leave after a tiff. Checked with Dave as I was leaving, "Are you okay?" He: "Well, we had a fight."

I, sorry to say, still a little raging: "I ask you not to empty the dishwasher, you put the dirties in with the cleans." But the real deal was that late this afternoon he was hungry. I gave him the remains of the lunch salad and pointed him to the crackers. Then I went back on the couch to read, a little hungry myself; I asked him to bring me some crackers. He, miffed: "This is my lunch!"

So unlike him. I bristled, "I made this lunch, I brought you the left over and showed you the crackers. You didn't want to share with me. I take care of you. I have the money (oh laws), I do everything for you."

Good gravy, get this woman out of here. Get her into a BMW with the sunroof open for the first time, (driving at reasonable speed), turn on the music, light a cigarette. And dive into dumb.

I really love dumb, clueless people. Sort of like pets. Sometimes you want to cuddle them, sometimes strangle.

It is clear to me I will be transported into the world where perfect humans live. Except I am not so perfect not good at spatial reckonings, have a hard time putting together three dimensional puzzles.

Plus, my elbow conks a bit when hammering a three inch nail through a two by four. Well, these are minor things. I used to be able to wrassle sheep, no small talent. Until that ewe I tried to load resisted and I fell, and tore open my knee. Ah, but she was glorious, eventually was loaded, and is now producing champions.

No regrets. What's next?

Chapter 30

APRIL 29, 2006

We buried Meggi today. In the path of the blowing apple blossoms and under the young Corkscrew Willow in the west side of the garden.

I woke to her panting around 5 am. She could not stand, or use her back legs at all. I wanted to wake Dave to help me get her down the steps outside. But realized he would be too confused and upset that I was crying, knowing we have to euthanize her. So I lifted her and carried her myself. Out to the deck, down the steps onto the lawn, where she could breathe fresh morning air. Sixty or seventy pounds of my Meggidoon.

In other days, I *would* have awakened Dave so we could work together, make the decision together, have coffee together, and cry together. Instead, I crawled back under the covers to hide from the inevitable. Just shove it away, hide reality for a little while longer.

No luck. I hand-fed her favorite food laced with aspirin — last-ditch effort to make her okay. At the least, relieve her pain.

Gave Dave only a quick glimmer of what was happening, said, "Meggi can't walk." Am I protecting him or denying him? I never know.

Took a shower and called Kathy at 9:30. She arranged for the vet to come here. I would not take her to the hospital for anything. Borrow the neighbors' gun before subjecting her to that stress.

And the rest was a movie: Meggi, the star, on her down comforter, her usual spot in our bedroom. Kathy on the floor petting and soothing, Simone bouncing between the bed and her mother's arms, all the while staring at Meggi intently, Dave sitting on the bed, the vet, Eric Kaiser, and his assistant, Anita. All in our bedroom.

And where am I? Here and not here. Comforting Meggi as I can, being comforted by Kathy, checking on Simone, who says, "Don't talk." And amazed that Dave is aware. He talks about the *good old dog.* Talks about Crater Clinic when it was small and how Doc Perry came out to take care of sick sheep and difficult births.

Meg fought the restriction, my one regret. So they gave her a sedative. She calmed down in ten minutes. Then it was sweet blue sleep. I told Simone, "She will be alive in my dreams."

Kathy reminded me Meggi loved a good tussle when we tried to groom her so she would have been distracted from the pain, wrassling one more time.

Dave and Kathy took turns digging the grave. We brought her out, curled like a sleeping puppy. Laid her in, threw on her a lot of the abundant mint stalks. Then the dirt. Simone planted an apple blossom on the top.

I am very sad. Take it back, take it back, rewind the film.

April 30, 2006

Last night Dave and I walked out into the garden and settled by Meggi's grave. It was a hellish day. Today I did not mind that she is not clacking on the bare floor in my office, imploring attention. I have not liked her breath in my face while I am reading on the couch. I had wished she did not need me so much in her later years.

But last night, we were mourning. And I, still today. Dave has said nothing, does not seem to notice.

In the garden together, last night we were in different roles than those of the last several years. More like it used to be. The back and forth, trying to be in each other's heads, finding out where the other is now.

When he began losing his wits, I withdrew from him a bit, knowing he couldn't understand me. In the past, two or three days a week we went out into the garden, or the lamb barn, smoked a joint, he with a beer, I with a scotch. And be in our place together. Wander the garden, I reveling in each plant, each placing, telling of plans. He nodding, learning, "daffodil," "pansy," as I learned, through him, Miles and Billy.

When the Alzheimer's struck, he could no longer drink because it accelerated his memory loss, and he slept all the time. He didn't believe me, but believed his doctor. So, we switched to TV and movies. I think now, perhaps that was too radical a switch. Our walks in the garden, I have those. He does not without me.

(Oh wow, there is a grosbeak on the feeder eating the corn suet. Oh my God, there are two more. I am never leaving here. They are supposed to be common, but we have never had one, let alone three.)

We are isolated from people, yes; from some of life, probably. But from basics of life, not at all. Never mind not discussing movies, we share our love of nature and of this singular place. The sheep are in heavy fleece so need shearing—another chance to be together in that shared part of our life. Our shearer retired last year. We will have Jack Decker come, the crazy man who can hold a live electric wire and not be hurt. Can't get too much more basic than that.

Today I am seeing *old* in everything. I now notice Mazie also has weak legs, Cindy panting more than usual, the rams ponderous on their ancient legs, Briquette yowling more before dawn.

In the mirror this morning I was a puffy mask of myself after hours of crying. Yes, for Meggi, yes for all of the dying that will be.

This morning, I looked for Mazie, wondering if she missed her friend. She was lying by Meggi's grave. A dead squirrel upon it. Her gift. Her sister. Did I cry? You bet.

Doth the Trumball
Fall to Darkness
Or the Mitty to the Briney?

Sluice sensed knowing
Uncovered pain,
Recovered, found

Yet comes the hope, Brine and Mitty
No shots to fire, reconciled?
Only the oysters will suffer.

Ophelia? What my pain too?
So little known.

Ophelia come to my heart,
No less raw than yours
I am not young.

Mitty, Briney come now, take me
Into cold hands
Yet I linger
Though I may regret,
I breathe on still.

I rage against the intrusion
You! Go away.

Chapter 31

May 1, 2006

Just finished *Blink: The Power of Thinking Without Thinking*. It is an absolutely fascinating discussion of our quick, unstudied, unanalyzed, unconscious decision making.

It brought to mind again my first encounter with Dave. How within seconds of meeting him at his door, asking for a donation, there was the flash of *I like this man*. It was not the love *at first sight* people talk about. *Like at first sight* may be stronger, longer lasting. That was forty-one years ago this summer. Wow!

One of the first studies cited in the book is about evaluations of relationships during a short interaction of the couple. Though the scientists may see something different, we pass with flying colors on the long marriage predictor. Well, of course, so does time – thirty years this June 26th.

Another part that struck me was an analysis of autistic persons' ability to get into the head of the other person, principally by reading their facial expressions, the nuances of their voices beyond the words. An example was the inability of the "subject" to follow the pointing of the other because the clues weren't sufficient.

This was so freaky to me, because this began happening to Dave a couple of years ago. Yesterday out in the garden we were weed-eating and mowing. He wanted to know where he should mow next. The explanation that he should mow where I had cut the grass to a shorter length did not register. I knew this, but kept trying.

Then I pointed. He kept looking at my face, trying, I assume, to glean an answer there. So I: "Don't look at my face, look to where I am pointing." He gazes around. He just does not get the pointing. So I walk him through it, the lawn, over and over, little bit by little bit. He wanted to do it, tried hard.

This sounds like a problem. And of course for us it is. But if the scientific community is tying these things together, the work being done in Autism research and Alzheimer's research might mesh and come to a common cure. From my pen to God's ears.

(Twelve goldfinches in the tray feeder, five on the vertical tube feeder, two doves on the branch, one redwing blackbird, 5:45 PM, May 1st, 2006. Recording just in case I need another career.)

Another of the clues that may contribute to solving this weird forgetting disease: in *The Song of Names*, the author Norman Lebrecht says, "Music, these rabbis must have known, clings to the brain like a barnacle."

Dave doesn't forget the music. The other day we were moving records. He saw a Chet Baker album, and said, "Ah, my man, Chet Baker." However, other than Miles or Dizzy, he does not always recognize the player as we listen. But Miles and Dizzy are trumpet players, his axe. Vocalists, though, he gets cold, even those like Neil Young, whom he had never heard until we were married.

Well, I am indulging in magical thinking. He often does, not always.

Then just now, watching *Casablanca*, the scene when Ilsa comes up to Rick's room, the point where he says, "Here's Looking at you kid," Dave laughed and said, "I knew that was coming soon, not just sure when."

What I would like to do is see if I can put some of the new memories into the place where the old ones reside.

My favorite scene in this movie is the singing competition. *La Marseillaise* is so powerful, the emotion so real. Acting in this scene? Not so much. A real tapping into hope.

We over sixty will not see the best human society can be, but I truly believe it will come. Notice how we keep looking?

Both loss and hope are part of my life now. Losing Meggi was hard, I am still sad, and will be for a while. I will not mourn the less because we have other loved animals. Right now Kitty Rings is trying to engage me, a bit more winsome than usual, not as demanding, though she just threw back my keyboard tray. There is no question she is tapping in into my emotions with empathy.

The oddest thing. I walked over to Meggi's grave this afternoon, and found a half-eaten squirrel on top of the mound. Not the same one as yesterday. The dogs regularly catch rodents. But it was weird, right on top center of the grave, again. In the heat, it had already started to putrefy, smelled, flies around. I picked it up and tossed it over the fence. Out of nowhere comes Mazie, with a manner and look that says, "What the Hell are you doing? I was giving that to my friend."

True story. Maybe the squirrel dropped from the sky, and Mazie just happened to walk by. I don't know, what do you think?

Right now, in this spring, the "cruelest months," the lilacs, blossoms born dead last year, are flush and raging this time, I re-vowed never to leave. The path I take through the grass to the barn, the seed heads of the softest of the grasses brushing on my bare legs, just so. The ground, now firm, hard.

That path I have walked for twenty years. What can another place give me? Will I go on a power walk with friends by the cemetery? Wander through North Mountain Park? And regret? And regret?

I will die with regrets, but not this one. If I can pick up from a dead weight my Meggi, 70 pounds or so, I can help a man out of a bed if necessary. I am already inured to cleaning up linens and clothes after his mishaps. If, at some point he doesn't recognize me any more, well, I recognize him. He will know my touch. My love.

May 2, 2006

This afternoon we drove into Gold Hill to take our mailings to the Post Office. Dave started talking about the Havurah Newsletter. He said, "This is a nice thing, fast, not crooked. It looks good, easy to read. Intelligent, knowledgeable people writing, getting others in there. Surprising for such a small town."

I was blown away. I: "This is what I have wanted to do." He: "Well, I think you are doing it."

Suddenly the off-memory glitches seem minor. I am becoming convinced my attitude has incredible influence. If this is all normal to me, it becomes normal, not stressful to him. When he needs to check on his next move with the mailings, he says, "Sorry to bother you, but..." It was never really an irritation because he is doing our business, and it needs to be done right. Now however, I am much more positive, let him know, hey, "We are doing this together, you have your job, I have mine. No sweat."

We go into the post office; Deborah says, "Hey you two, we were just talking about you." I: "What about?" Shirley: "I won the high sales for last week." We all chuckle, I say, "Oh yeah, well, our buying 1700 stamps at once, that certainly gave you an edge." The amount we bought last Friday, and today bringing in the stamped mailings, is our joint effort. The work we do to make a living, makes a living for them.

They call me Ms. Montgomery. That's a little scary.

This kind of exchange is so much what it is all about. I will be happy, surely comfortable, anywhere. Dave likes his familiars. At the pharmacy last week, we were both greeted. All our people know his condition. Nancy: "Hi Dave, hi Michelle." Back in the car, Dave: "Yeah, those are my girls." Ashland is big town compared to tiny Gold Hill. Though the Havurah people in Ashland, our circle of friends, will understand how to keep Dave within the group and familiar.

A simple village is what we need. When I was young, we lived on the outskirts of Palm Springs, then a small town. My brother and sister, Chip, Kathy and I would go out into the desert, built a fire, take a piece of bread with ketchup and pretend it was beans and tortilla, pretend we were cowboys.

Kathy and I rode horses out into the desert once a week, into the sand, I was ten, she six. Why would we ever be afraid of anything now? Dave relies on me to protect him, our roles reversed from our early marriage. If he wanders, which he does even out here, someone will recognize him.

It is hard for me to believe I am not going to live forever and still have all choices before me. Actually, I do not believe it. Sure, I *know* it, but what is knowing against *believing*? And the corollary: if you are not here today, you sure as heck are not going to be here tomorrow.

I am writing and writing tonight to get out of the sadness of Meggi, dancing and dancing to be alive. Listening to *Hand Jive* on Napster for Heaven's sake. Well, what could be better? Grab, keep grabbing at life. Stop death. Stop that needle in her arm, stop the quiet, slow blue death of the drug that ends it all.

May 4, 2006

Yesterday, Kathy said, "What do you think I moved out here for?"

She came over while the carpet installers were here—both Dave and I were stressed. We tried to move out most of the furniture before they came. Beds, lamps, side tables, all the clothes in the guest room closet, everything on the floor in my office. The computer and the mega attachments later, phone, cords, and on and on.

"Why didn't you call me to help?" I: "I didn't want you to have to get up too soon." The truth is, she has so much to take care of on her own, Simone, the #1 priority for us both, and she now starting a new business.

Truth is, by now we are exhausted. The guys did not finish yesterday, had to come back this morning.

Neither Dave nor I do well with chaos, disorganization, disruption. In the midst of this, Thursday morning, trash day, trucks blocking the driveway, we had to take up the trash. We now do it together, can in the back of the Beemer (pickup out of gas as usual). Dave was so, so slow, as though a zombie. His every move was slow; he was concentrating, trying to get some clue. A clue of what he was to do next. That happens to him when there is too much input or stimulation, a protection really.

Back to yesterday: Two young bucks here, Ben and Brendan. Kathy and Simone coming to keep our crazy company. They were short carpet for the hall. Kathy dealt with Lowe's. She had to, I was close to tears. Just as she dealt with the vet when I was in tears.

I am being taken care of. I am supposed to be the caretaker. I to her: "I just want my normal life back." She: "What is normal when you have a husband with Alzheimer's?" Good point.

We ate peanuts and crackers for dinner. Dave's bed in the guest room was not there, out on the deck along with its mate. Came back to our bed, once again, fully clothed. *Oh laws*. I prefer skin, but, it *was* a little chilly.

Woke early for the next onslaught. This time, four guys. Dave and I hid in the bedroom. He read the paper, I finished a depressing book. Almost fell asleep, but for the raucous fun happening out in the living room. These guys, talking beer, booze, bikes, and shotguns. And, as sweet as they could be to us. No strangers come into this house anymore. Strangers are greeted at the gate, come through the gate as not-strangers.

They brought back all the furniture, placed it just so, just nice. And, the most amazing thing, fixed the broken leg on our dining room table. The older guy, Richard, saw the problem, said, "You must have a can of nuts and bolts out there in the garage." Well, of course, we did. He said, "Every farm does." I brought the bolts. My boys were spending a bit of time giving to a neighbor, someone who needed the leg on their table fixed. So easy to find the Good.

I think I have discerned why people like me. It is because I like them. Yesterday when the guys were leaving, they paused at the door, and we talked a bit. Later Kathy said, "What was that, why didn't they just leave...out, out." I: "Everyone who comes here does that." I am curious about who they are, want to say, "Hey, you cool." We are the same, the workers and I.

(Oh laws, that crazy llama Dempsey, jumped the fence to eat apple tree leaves, now drinking from the birdbath, Dave going out on the deck, thinking he can do something. I: "Hey, he got in, he can get out." Then the conversation with Black Magic who is irate today is not an alfalfa day: "Hey, you ate yesterday, there is a lot of grass, and you are a sheep.")

So now, my house is becoming my mother's. This edible color green carpet, this simplifying. Kathy and I agreeing our paintings need to come down. Oh the mourning for that. Too wild, too free. Peace now. Calm. Maybe I can turn the garage into a gallery. Already her crazy nude women painting from her Senior show is on the back wall. (What does the UPS man think?)

Will I really replace my favorite two works with a Renoir print in a Rocco frame? Maybe. Something I won't have to think about now.

I just looked down and saw I have blood on my fingertip, blood on my cigarette tip, that little salty taste. Kids know that taste. Where did it come from? Ain't mysteries grand?

My father sliced his wrists with a large knife. I wonder if he spent time deciding which knife to use. He was a great cook; I cannot imagine he did not make a choice. My step-sister/cousin, Roxanne, knows which knife it was. I will have to ask her. She picked it up. Threw the cover over him. The police were not happy campers. I suppose they thought there might have been a crime. Well, of course there was.

She called us quickly; the police did not let her use the phone once they got there. I called sister Kathy; we were out on the next plane.

I am thinking about this because of Meggi. *That Rewind the Tape* feeling. Take it back, take it back.

It was ten years ago this fall: driving down the driveway after *Kol Nidre,* Yom Kippur first evening, full of joy, singing all the way home.

So indelibly printed: Dave coming out from the garage entrance, coming up to the car; "Roxanne just called, your father took his own life."

If I could take this one moment back, everything would be okay again.

∽

Tonight, Erev Yom Kippur
Take from me my sins, Hashem

I watch the sun set
Into the day of confession
The beginning of the pure new year

See me nevermore, though
At that temple
From which I returned,
Dancing and singing
Ten years ago

To hear of my father's death:
"Your father has taken his life."
And some of mine.

I light the yartseit candle
I listen for the answer
No answer, only tears.

∽

Chapter 32

MAY 5, 2006

By last night we still had not gotten the beds back into the guest room, Dave's refuge. I felt him missing around three am and went to look for him; he was wandering—shirt, no pants, and lap blanket around his shoulders. He was looking for his cap. I found it quickly and we went back to bed.

In the morning when he got up, I asked him how he had slept. He wasn't sure. I: "Last night you were wandering." He: "Yes, I was looking for the thing that would make me happy."

Amen, brother. A cap. All he needed was a cap to be happy. Is that a good thing or a bad thing? S'pose it depends where yur head's at.

Me? I like complexity. Throw it at me. I am just waiting for the real test. Every blast proves me. Results are what count—as they say, it's not how you start, but how you finish. I plan on finishing well. No knife for me, leaving anguished children. Though we all knew it would happen that way, my Daddy.

The much lesser story is whether or not I will survive this new carpeting. It is so clean, no boots, no garden shoes. Panic about possible cat pee if the door to the garage is not open during the night (Dave and I have different ideas about that).

And, the real panic, my mother's approval comes through loud and clear; "Yes, perfect color, yes, get all that wild art out of here, yes, good, make Dave take his boots off. No, put the dog food and water outside." A voice still, though she has been dead for eleven years.

"And for heaven's sake, take Roxy's painting out of your office." True, it says more than any of us want to hear—an Airstream planted on the sand, a huge rabbit, conejo, running across the dunes, the luring ocean. Titled: *Ephemeral*. Roxy is a little bit crazy. Sometimes a little bit crazy is just what we need.

My gorgeous Kitty Rings came in for a petting a minute ago, looking even more beautiful on this perfect green carpet which highlights her cream and grey fur. She is the one we rescued from a friend's shotgun, just an extra barn cat to him. Why am I here rather than in Darfur with the Red Cross? Comforting a cat rather than a small child?

Get thee to a nunnery Michelle, you must repent your lack of perfection!!! *Hah, begone scolding voice, no one tells me what to do.*
Well, yes, I could do better. Oh, I don't know, maybe. So tired, so tired of being in charge. It is no wonder my imagination flies in all directions—to capture and bring home that which is a comfort and allows a bit of escape.

Under my grandmother's dinner table there was a little button she could press and the maid would come in to take whatever direction Grandma came up with, usually a request to clear the plates for the next course, to bring in the finger bowls with flowers floating.

It took me the longest time to find out how the maid knew to come in at the exact time Grandma wanted her. I want one of those buzzers to call someone to come in and take my place for a little while.

May 7, 2006

When I am fragile it doesn't take much to nudge me off balance. Today I read two articles in *The New Yorker*, one about an American Muslim in prison for life, possibly wrongly accused and convicted, and the other about the schism in the Episcopal Church over the election of a gay Bishop. As I read I became increasingly depressed: *no, no, no. Stop.* Stop all adherence to a particular religion for one month (Buddhists and Hindus excepted). Look at the real word, stop this nonsense. This is not about God. Get a grip. I want to shake your skinny assed testosterone flooded bodies to Kingdom Come. There you won't be so much up on your high horse! St. Peter, St. Ali Baba, or St. Yitzhak, saying to you: "Hey dude, you weren't listening. This is a story about love...you know, widows and orphans and such, your brothers and sisters, doing unto others and all that."

We are both very tired, temporarily broken down by the last week—weariness makes both of us fragile. It started last Saturday with the death of Meggi, then the moving furniture, the garden work, the onslaught of people here for two days to put in the carpet. And, yesterday, for me, Simone's birthday party on Kathy's wide lawn, sloping to the pond where the first wild ducks are returning.

A perfect party, though draining that one last bit of energy because I had to race around the big lawn to hide the treasures. The treasure hunt, the kids frosting the cupcakes, so many kids and parents to join the celebration—all Kathy's planning. I am so proud of her—what a good mother and lovely human being she is.

To see the Dads at these parties, she also hosted an Easter egg hunt last month, has been a surprise to me. I don't remember men being at my kids' parties, or my childhood parties. Things are changing, for the better it seems. The fathers really engaged with their kids, big men holding little babies. Nice.

So, the word is out. Studies have shown this is what makes us happy, the little day-to-day things. I sure hope my tax dollars didn't pay for that—so obvious. At the party yesterday, a tiny girl kept trying so hard to walk between her father's hands and mine. What smiles she gave me: "I know you, you are that woman who likes kids." Back and forth. Another child spotted me, a little chubby brown baby, crawled over and climbed into my lap. Sure I want a perfect house. But much more I want to pack my life full of memories.

The big stuff is a background blur. The reality, the true happiness is that trail of rams moving out to the west pasture; the birds glad we had finally gotten their seed; Etta James singing *I'd rather go blind than see you walk away from me*; my husband fed and content for now; green, green all over. I am not blessed. I am lucky. There is absolutely no reason I can discern why I should be here and not that child in Darfur. Jeeze, I hope I have done well enough this time so next time I can come back as a clone of Mother Teresa.

At different times my sisters have called me in tears and anguish about their concern for the world, the people of the world. They list on and on about the sufferings. I recognize depression. I have it. Under control with an antidepressant. (I love the directness of that label.) As always I say: "Pick one. Do something about that one. You cannot save them all."

Perhaps because I am a child of privilege I am relieved to be tested. I was calm today when Dave attempted to put anti-freeze into the lawn mower. He was fixated on the mower, wanting to mow, to be active and useful. I tried to explain, "We have no gas, GASOLINE, for the mower. Your job is to cut down the high grass out by the fence with the weed-eater." Oh my.

Test me, test me. I am ready. Leave alone my children and grandchildren. But fire, flood, wolves howling (no, strike that, that would be a gift), nothing will daunt me. I will find what I need in a hawk soaring, in a little worm crawling. Well, actually, worms don't crawl, but you get the idea. Touching on and experiencing all that is good, magical even, keeps me centered. I am then a child of more privilege than comes from money. Whenever I funny-talk to Dave, "I want to be rich!" he still replies, "We are." Indeed.

May 8, 2006

Absolutely sublime day. Simone's fifth birthday. Kathy called early to ask if I wanted to be with them when she opened her presents. Brushed my teeth, but otherwise, what you see is what you get. Kathy and I had such a nice quiet time to talk before Simone and Roxy woke up. I went to look in on her a couple of times. What is more beautiful than a child sleeping well?

Back home by nine-thirty to begin a day of putting things back together. Finally energy and order are returning.

This morning Dave and I watched news, then Jon Stewart. I had left him earlier with the News at his request. Came back to him napping. The first of three or four today. A bit worrisome. He mowed a little, but very little. He used to have such stamina. Still has the drive to be active, but his body rarely agrees to do all he planned. We each have our annual physicals in two weeks. Maybe a clue.

I can see I am still in partial denial. (Oh no, will I have to go back over the course again? Or can I come back to the Rogue River and forget de' Nile?) What I keep saying is, "He is only seventy-six." I sometimes forget the Alzheimer's part. Well, he is my man-child, I don't think of him as diseased, only about how he is in the world right now, at any given moment.

Example: Just now, he came down the hall, toothpick in mouth, watch cap in hand. I keep track when he is wandering. Asked if his head was cold, did he need his cap. He: "No, I was just looking for someplace to put it." I took it from him, tossed it through the guestroom door — it hit the wall and landed on the chair next to his other favorite cap. He: "She good, she really good." I: "Do you think I can make it with the Lakers?" He: "Oh yeah."

Play, play, play. Laughing is the elixir.

May 9, 2006

Trapped by beauty, trapped by love, trapped by *am I allowed, really, to do this every day?*

The lilacs are sublime. Reminds me of the Kismet garden of the lovers. I feel drugged. Drugged by Spring. Drugged by perfection. Drugged by the inaction of all that is still to be done.

Yesterday I asked Kathy, "What do you suppose would happen to us if I did nothing? Would we be sent to a homeless shelter?" She: "No, I think you would just be sitting outside your gate on the road." Hey, cool reality check. Never happen of course. But still…

What if I were to become a crazy woman with long white hair and long toenails? Missing teeth. Telling it like it is. Claw like fingers, grasping at passing children, cackling.

I was thinking of becoming an actor, joining one of those little theater groups. I can easily lose myself into another. Practicing accents a little. Country gal and high English are my favorites. Think I could do Irish and Scottish with a little practice. White trash, my alter ego, for sure. Wait scratch that. Well, maybe, haven't come up with an alternative. The gum, the slouch, the *fuck you* attitude—I already have the ponytail. Or my beloved adolescent girls: "Yeah, well whatever," and then slide my eyes and turn my head, chin dropping.

Okay, country gal wins: I just went out to check on Dave and picked up a squirrel skull on our new carpet; not fresh but still some fur.

"Hey hon, didja see what the dog brung in?" "Nah punkin, wha' was it?" "Dern squirrel them dogs was chasin' yestaday." "Got enuf meat on so's we can eat it?"

⁓

High English: "Oh my, Skuzzims has brought us a gift. Good girl, good girl, what have you brought to Mommy? Now, that is so sweet. But gardner must take it out and cook will take you to the kitchen for a special treat.

⁓

Irish/Scottish: "Durn col commin' agin wi' the rascal bin routin in th' garden. Gud col. Gi' back to the kitchen, the ma gi' yu somethin."

⁓

Valley Girls, aka all current adolescents: "Oh yuk."

Chapter 33

MAY 10, 2006

Ah yes, Neil Young is up and at 'em again...downloading his new album: *Living With War*. He is raging. Giving a voice. Aren't we sick of this? The war, yes, but this weird administration? I do not have a huge complaint about Republican philosophy, when honest about goals. But why do they choose such peculiar leaders? Know-nothings, crooks and space cases?

Oh, really, I do not have time or energy for this. (Though if not I, who?)

We settled down tonight for our five o'clock *Law and Order*. I asked Dave to get the peanuts. He brought me a spoon: "Is this what you want?" Tracked it back to the spoon being on the counter when he went to get the peanuts. Tracked it in my supposing, he would not have been able to track back.

I want to enfold him in my arms as a comforting Nanny would do, "Ah, little wee bairn, yu'v lost yur wey joust a bit. Neve' mine, ma will tek gud care of yu. Cummon in and hev sum tea."

How deep do I go into becoming slightly crazy myself in this topsy-turvy world we've made?

It would be unlike me to rely on an imaginary being for help, but if I did, it might say, "Ah my dear sweet gurl. Yu know how truly I luv thee. So I must tell ya true, yu must keep on thy track. Neever let it scare ya. Ah, my little one, I em so sad for yur hurt. Jest as you burried Meggi, yu will bury others. Yu will survive. E'en if yu don't want."

"Ah my dear" yourself, Mr. Smarty Pants God. You are taking away my man for no good reason he is a good man, has always been a good man. Do not sacrifice him in order to test me. Whatever are you thinking? Yeah, yeah, I am supposed to use this for some greater good—mind telling me what that is?"

May 11, 2006

Listening to the new Neil Young and dealing with tiny things like these full ashtrays, is in this moment of feeling blue, just one more burden among the many emotional ones. I am truly afraid Iran will bomb Israel. I am truly afraid those I love will be harmed. I am truly afraid my two remaining roosters will be grabbed by the coyotes, my two remaining dogs will die, and my cats will go to the attic and die, as Mickey did, or under the deck, as Jack did.

Being alive, even in privileged circumstance, has its cost. Ah, Janis, "Freedom's just another word for nothing left to lose."

Love and attachment has a huge cost. Dave today, trying to work the weed eater around the rocks. Instead, he moved out to the lawn, mowing it short with the weed-eater. I had to take him from that and put him onto another project. There is something obsessive-compulsive about his actions these days—once he decides on an action he incessantly repeats it whether appropriate or not. It hurts my heart to watch him. I weep at the inevitability of huge losses—of him, of our home.

Or perhaps we can begin to know freedom when we can accept the fact that we will lose and continue nonetheless to love. An ultimate advantageous disadvantage transcending necessity. But it takes looking honestly at what is.

May 12, 2006

This winding down of our lives together is so multidimensional His, mine, and ours. And others also. Tonight I realized I cut his chicken for him before I gave him his plate. When did that start? He is certainly capable, but it upsets me to see him awkward—awkward in balancing the plate on his lap. We have been having dinner while watching TV for the last couple of years. My choice really. I am afraid of dinner table conversations with him now—trapped into the scariness of our mutual incomprehension.

I'm an absolute bitch tonight. Whatever happened to Shabbat dinners, making Challah in the afternoon? Gone, for now, anyway. Kathy and Simone would gladly come, but I have zilch for meeting responsibilities beyond the immediate all consuming ones.

On the other hand, remembering what we did/could do in the garden a couple of years ago feels not so different from now. Dave has much less stamina, but I have more patience and do not resort to the sciatica born of frustration I had then. It is not problem for me now to walk out every few minutes to re-direct or help.

And help he needs. He is a compass needle, north is the flower bed. It is a given for me now he will go there no matter how much I implore him to stay away. There are huge areas of tall grass for him to work on, but no, the flower bed draws him and his lawn mower. I am not completely convinced his passive resistance of days gone by is not still operative. After all, his basics have not changed.

Hence my bitchiness at his disintegration when he took his dirty dinner plate and wiped it with a towel. I am far from a germ freak, even a cleanliness freak, but I am starting to inspect the dishes that come out of the cupboard.

Maybe it is time to run the dishwasher (I rebel against running it until completely full). I look in it, and what do I see but more chaos than John Nash's mind. This man who used to be so orderly lost it along the way. This re-denial of mine is disturbing to say the least. I'm buying time, "Just another year." Or two. I absolutely must see that transplanted tree peony bloom. Those two new forsythia. And the wisteria on the back deck.

This view from my office, out to the south pasture, the Shabbat sun setting, this spring grass, all green and golden. How can I leave this? Truly, how can I leave this?

I remember a movie about a semi-crazy woman who lived in the woods and for some reason had her grandson staying with her. They played wonderful make-believe. Many times I hope I will get to be that crazy woman. After all, what has our sane humanness gotten us? The awareness of pain, loss and death. Consider the lucky worm. Being clueless and narcissistic seems less painful.

I want to be Gloria Swanson in that most perfect of scenes, Norma Desmond: "All right, Mr. DeMille, I'm ready for my close-up." I am Norma Desmond in my self-conscious drama. People think more of me, my 'trial' than they need. It is just my life now. I am brave, beautiful, dramatic, frustrated, life-lover, mean, selfish, sad, happy. Oh, yeah, also loving and creative.

May 13, 2006

Today he was so tired he took several naps and had a hard time putting words to his thoughts. Or so I guessed, as he spoke so mumblety I couldn't understand. Usually I nodded or laughed as seemed appropriate. Apparently that worked.

Our evenings are routine. We put on the TV, I bring peanuts, then dinner, which is sometimes only chicken nuggets, cheese and crackers. I bop in and out, writing, and then checking on him. Last night we watched a *Law and Order* about a young man who committed murders while under the influence of a cult leader.

The exposition of the seduction, the entanglement into the cult was so like what Thomas and I experienced when we went to Lan Jordan for help putting our marriage back on track. Actually, Thomas never saw it. He had the money, he was the one seduced. When I rebelled, particularly for the protection of my children, she made sure Thomas would be stuck to her. Oh, she knew so well his insecurity, his F-scale (fascism scale: charts willingness to bow to authority, and need to be the authority). He chose the cult over his family, never acknowledging, perhaps not even knowing, what he was doing.

So many religions are like that. Or some of the parts of the overarching 'faith.' Being raised an Episcopalian, a Protestant denomination of particularly liberal and broad interpretations of the faith, I don't feel strictured. The rites were heavy on robes and candles, stained glass. But you could say whatever you wanted. The sermons, usually based on a Bible portion, sometimes one of the Gospels, but often as not, the Old Testament, were messages, not orders.

Certainly easy to segue into Judaism. But not Messianic. Here and now. Do good, be good. Ah, and resist temptation.

May 14, 2006

As I watched the last episode of *West Wing* just now, I felt as though I was losing some of my best friends. Was teary throughout. Seven years. The first four with Sorkin in charge were the best, but the remaining three still made it for me. This is craziness, what Ray Bradbury predicted. My life more involved with the goings on at a fictional White House than real life.

Today, Kathy, Simone, and I went to my niece Gemini's baby shower. I awoke to the yowling of Briquette at 5:30. Was able to sleep again until 6. But then, the stomach upset, the feeling puny. I recognize it so well: *You want an excuse not to go.* But I must, I love these nieces of mine, and my sister. Still, hoping Kathy will call and say she is sick also, we cannot go. My children have diagnosed "mild agoraphobia." It is not really that, I just sometimes get overwhelmed by the unknown.

The party was in the garden of the Ashland Creek Inn, such a beautiful spot. And yes, there were lots of people there I did not know, or sort of knew, but had nothing to say to. Not my family of course. My joy. It was just that it was so crowded, energy sapping, draining my reservoir. Every once in a while I asked Kathy, "Can we go yet?" She inclines, tilts, her head, meaning: if you want, but do we really want to go?

It got better, but I talk crazy, manic, mouth before brain. Have I always been like this? No wonder I prefer writing. Apparently who I am is endearing to my kin. We laugh and laugh. I am nuts around people. Forget the name of my only granddaughter, and who is related to whom.

Looking into someone's face sweeps me away, pulls me in, I am so fascinated. It is intolerable to the part of me that wants to be alone. But captivating to me the searcher: look at her, that face full of action, laugh lines, grey hair worn with pride, those words she is saying.

Look at him, the way he holds his body, the being here at the baby shower, though he is the only man, a gay man, Daniel. To whom do I gravitate? The one who has something to say. Do I wish life could be on e-mail? A little bit. But a person? A real person? That is truly trippy.

Came home to Dave, seems fine, but he did not eat the lunch I had clearly labeled, nor read the paper. Sitting watching CNN, which was on when I left four hours before.

May 15, 2006

I just heard the funniest thing: "If you are going to be stupid, you have to be strong." What does that mean?

And yesterday at Gemini's shower I learned what it means to be "beside yourself." Thank God for my dear ones who can look me in the eye, hold my hand, and calm me.

This morning the feeling resurfaced perhaps because my multi-tasking was extreme—I looked at myself and laughed. *This is so silly, who does this?*

Woke up looking out on that wonderful south view. After the peek out the window into the possibility of the day, the *Modah Anee*, my morning prayer of thanksgiving, my remembering the joy of life.

I saw the ram's water pail was full. Remembered I had filled it, Black Magic and Fatty Patty's also, cleaned them both. Gave me a jolt, a good rush, back onto the pillow, with a smile. Isn't it funny how we smile to ourselves? Okay, I have taken care of them, not something to do today. I done good.

But then, wake up! Get the coffee, feed the animals, work on the Newsletter, check Sandy's business, check Quicken...set the sprinklers, the deep watering...do as much as you can before Dave wakes up. Get that conflict out of here. Not possible to do entirely. But give it my best shot.

It happened when Kathy, Simone and I were walking along the creek, Simone's druthers, drawing us farther into the wild, keeping her protectors close. I looked out on to the neighbors' property... so much open land and trees. The properties that surround us with open land are better even than my hope for living on 100 acre. Surrounding us is at least 100 acres.

I went into that space. Not intentionally. Removed, standing back, beside myself, above myself looking on. Stoned. Stoned with life. Into that space today, during the multi-tasking I saw myself dragging hose, setting sprinklers.

Coming back to do the office work, to feed my beloved, who has forgotten he had lunch. So gave him more food, and restricted him to five from seven Pepsis a day. He growled slightly.

The elk were here today! Not the whole herd. What I saw through the binocs were two does and a calf. No worries, the whole herd will be back soon, they do not leave their kin alone.

Chapter 34

MAY 23, 2006

I really do not know what I am doing here.

I envy the sheep and the llamas, the chickens. They are here, they eat, sleep, play, had sex (before all the females were gone), and they die. It seems so pointless.

Various philosophers have said our goal is pleasure, optimizing pleasure, minimizing pain. The definition of pleasure can be broad, includes altruism. I have no issue with that, seems a biological given. However, goal and purpose are not the same.

Yesterday I cancelled my doctor's appointment for my yearly physical. Said I was not well. How odd is that, not going to the doctor because you are sick? I cannot move, go anywhere.

I do not understand why I am so stuck in indecision. Except, there is so much to do. But no more than there was ten years ago. In fact, our life in most senses is much better, more settled and organized. Of course "most senses" is nothing if the important part is gone.

I grab and grab at making order, creating purpose for each day. Today, I made some order of my music library. Tomorrow, I will start cataloguing our video cam films, maybe even transferring some to tape.

Most men lead lives of quiet desperation and go to the grave with the song still in them. —— Henry David Thoreau

But why? Why live at all? Perhaps to sing that song.

When you've thought you've lost everything, you find out you can always lose a little more. ——— Bob Dylan

One foot in front of the other, that's the way to go. *Buck up Mickey.* My father and grandfather's nickname for me, I would allow no one else to use it.

This morning I walked up the road to get the paper, determined not to be swamped. Tonight downloaded Johnny Otis' *Willie and the Hand Jive.* But cried while dancing.

It is all so silly, so dramatic, this being human business. Consider the lucky worm; I seem to be continually doing that. No, better, the lucky caterpillar!

I want my daddy back; he would know what I was talking about. He also asked the larger questions. He was also trapped in a life he felt was like wading through quick sand. His? much different from mine...more about wasted dreams.

I have my dream. What I do not have any longer, or fully, is the partner in that dream. But is that true? No, he is here with me, loving the land and the animals along with me. Perhaps I am questioning something else, again. The cities, the opera, the museums, the openings which we can no longer share.

Tomorrow Simone comes, my joy. Worth life, living for.

May 25, 2006

I just called Lowe's to find out what is happening with the hall carpeting that has not been installed because of mis-measuring. (Oh, Miss Measuring, nice to make your acquaintance.)

The operator asked to what department I should be directed. I said I did not know, but conveyed the problem, at her request (amazing). I told her I had received a message my "product" had arrived and I was to pick it up.

She laughed and said, "No, that is way too heavy for you to carry."

I: "Thank heavens for after-hours people, they understand."

She, chuckling: "Okay sweetie, I'll direct you to flooring."

So what I get is if I can allow others to be in the world for free, I might as well accept I can be here too. I am overwhelmed by entitlement. Hence, accepting the "slings and arrows of outrageous fortune."

And what could be more outrageous than finding out your spouse has been losing his mind for half your marriage?

Well, I don't regret that I accepted an education, a private school education, and the enormous skill of Miss Carnes, teacher extraordinaire.

But see, that is just it. If I didn't have a grandmother who could pay the tuition of Marlborough, whatever would have become of me? Probably selling apples, or matchsticks, on the street. (Oh good gravy drama queen, how much fun you have with this.)

Okay, what I decided this morning: *You, madam, not only accept, but applaud the life of others. So grow up my darling little guilt tripper. Just accept the gift and say, "Thank You." Any thing else is less than polite. And, after all, you were taught to curtsy.*

This morning I went to see my doctor Jean for my yearly exam so full of anxiety my legs shook in the stirrups. Before that, a wonderful conversation as she and I always have, this time about sailing, how Dave and I made love while sailing in Santa Monica Bay. She: "On auto pilot?" No, I am the captain, holding the tiller, maintaining our direction. Just for fun. To see if we could.

Dave is slowly sliding, but never misses a chance for a one-liner: Kathy tonight asking if he had cut his hair: "No, I just think so much that my brain is getting bigger."

Right now *Willie and the Hand Jive* is playing. But tonight I am laughing, not crying.

May 28, 2006

Dave's warm-up this morning:

"Well, I guess that's just about it." Pause...

I: "Oh yeah, what?"

He: "It's a long way to Tipperary."

Then we listened to orchestral pieces, one an exuberant Wagner (yeah, yeah, I know it's not allowed. Many Jews do not listen to Wagner, but hey, it's the music, right?).

The piece ended. After a couple of seconds, he said, "No applause? What is it with this town?" Oh my God, how fun these laughs are. He, getting his bearings, me getting his.

From the start of watching *Capote* last night, I had this weird perception of how tight within their skin each character is. Very visceral. Very acknowledged. This is each of us. Tied within our skin, bound—forever inside ourselves.

The drive to reach the ecstatic is understandable. The drive to accept the ordinary, the mundane, is understandable. The drive to dissolve the boundaries is understandable. At least to me. I talked to E last night. So much good stuff. We talked about our men, hers in his mid-eighties, just put into the grave. I talked about the salve of cuddling, erasing separation.

So, the *Capote* thing. It may have intentionally been filmed that way, well must have been. The isolation was so palpable.

I cannot imagine a life without art.

I cannot imagine a life without those who grow potatoes.

May 29, 2006

Well, I see I am not dead yet.

Tracked down the songs on the really choice video of a man dancing to various cuts of *The Evolution of Dance*. Kathy knew them all. I knew only the Elvis and the Chubby Checker. She was astonished I had never heard Michael Jackson. She was insistent I must have, sang the song, *Billy Jean*. I thought it was about the tennis player Billy Jean King, so I down loaded it. Definitely appealing, good dance, but what is that voice?

So went on to AC-DC, *You Shook Me All Night Long*. Wow, really liked it. So out of the dark ages you come Grandma.

Might next download, if you can believe it: *Tumthumping*, by Chumbawabe. (Well, as it turns out, iTunes never heard of it.) If I had broadband, the men in white coats would have to come and take me away. Another reason not to leave here.

Art is the most intense mode of individualism that the world has known.

It's Oscar Wilde again. One of these days I might read something other than his bit of wisdom. It continues to amuse me I think I have anything to say that might be of interest to others.

Yesterday at Rainey's, as happens again and again, I appreciate the woman at the check-out, not the same woman each time, but the same. This beautiful face, this connecting. This person who is a clerk at a corner store in Sams Valley. Alive.

I am becoming fascinated with faces. Remember those incredible portraits of Georgia O'Keefe her lover Steiglietz created? Well, of course, he did not create her face.

My favorite of hers: *Clouds,* conceived while flying, to Chicago I think, and perhaps resides in the museum there. Maybe New York. Twenty-four feet long, a marvel of imagination and dedication.

May 30, 2006

Well everyone knows something, even if it is only the name of their dog. Whoops, maybe not—since Meggi died, Mazie has become M*azie, Meggi, Mazie.*

Gardeners *do* know something. It would be a big surprise to me if most gardeners did not see the same metaphors I do. Today, pulling and pulling, digging at weeds, ignoring time, pain: get the unwanted out...now!

Inordinate attention to the white aster encroached on by the grass and the wild violets: leave my baby alone! She gives me joy. Finding a hosta I planted two years ago, thought lost, still trying to thrive, and also encroached upon. Damn the grasses, the wild violets. Protect the unprotected, I am woman, I am strong. Most of the time.

And, once again, consider the humble worm. I stopped to move it before I confronted a nasty blackberry vine, afraid I might step on her.

Well, I guess the story is: I am the big cheese. I get to decide which lives and which dies. Though those blackberries fight so hard you have to admire them. I fight them bare handed, blood on the hands. Strikes me as a fair fight. I won this one. For now only—they shall return.

June 4, 2006

There comes a time when you realize you are completely alone. I took a class on it once.

One of my more weird experiences. The professor just sat there. He said nothing. It was up to us to create, define the session. Very scary, scary to have an expected structure turned upside down, like my life now.

It was a small seminar, ten or so people around the table. He was demonstrating the theory of a psychologist who believed that we have to recognize the fact of our being: "We are born alone, we die alone."

I wonder if Dave is feeling more and more alone. Isn't a pure definition of "alone" the absence of any connection? He is losing his connection to the world most inhabit—and to the one I inhabit.

His doctor once related how one of his patient's whole life was within them selves only. She would grab the nurses fiercely if they touched her body. The doctor explained this is often part of the last stage—any disruption that intrudes on her reality is a threat.

June 5, 2006

I am beginning to realize that Dave's space is not a bad one for him other than occasional frustrations.

Tonight I was on the phone with Kathy. He asked if she had been traveling. He remembers that she used to travel. He does not remember that she was here day before yesterday.

The lawn still hasn't been entirely mowed so he kept on it. Once again he works to maintain his usual routine, his way of being in the world. Nothing I said could convince him not to mow in the deep grass because it was such hard work. I wonder if he is confused by the process or by my words; if only by my words, I must let him be. He got so hot working with the long grass binding the blade. And still he headed back to where I suggested he shouldn't, again his compass arrow going to the north of whatever is in his head. I can only guess he gets satisfaction from the challenge.

Every activity requires a nap break so that on some days he spends more time sleeping than being in our lives.

(There are so many finches on the feeders outside the window, chattering and singing, that I can barely concentrate. Birds show no respect to artists.)

Such good work in the garden today. Reflects my state. An uncontrolled, untended, garden makes me crazy. Oh those damn metaphors again. Wonder if anyone will know what I am talking about.

One of those lovely men dropped into my life today. Kathy's referral, Larry Neil. Someone to mow the smaller areas, the sheep yards, around the trees, creek area. He wanted to also mow the pastures.

I am so excited. What I thought could not be done because of the cost, is a nip and tuck by someone who lives up the road and tends to his own property with ease. I am in love with Sams Valley. I am in love with all these dear country men who want to take care of me.

June 6, 2006

Well, that sometimes causes problems. The "taking care of" and the testosterone combo. Larry came here this morning as promised. Fixed the road, all the potholes out. Then came back after lunch to mow the sheep yards and parts of the east of the driveway, and (without my asking) the stuff down by the creek.

When he finished, he asked if I want any more mowing done. I guide him into the garden. I know that I told him explicitly where he was to go but, macho on tractor, wanting to help the damsel by doing more, everything she would wish, went on a tear and accidentally mowed down my young forsythia, part of a wild rose, and of course, dontcha know, part of my Virgin's Bower.

I question myself for being a user of that testosterone. But not sure where my liking, loving even, 'the other' and my (possibly) manipulative charm separate. On the other hand, I charm women also. Oh give it up Michelle, this whole conversation is *narishkeit*. You am what you am.

June 7, 2006

Dave slept most of the day. I was in the garden at eight. We live parallel and consecting lives. (Apparently there is no such word as consect. I, disbelieving the dictionary just now and looking skeptical, got Dave's attention so he asked what the problem was. His answer: "Hey nobody will know." Hey, I'll take it and call it good.) It is those moments of complete comprehension and expansive thinking that gives me hope for many more years together at this tolerable stage.

Though my love never wavers, it is nourished by the sparks of reminders of how he used to be.

June 8, 2006

All that sleep was good for Dave. Very up and with it today.

And I? Going more and more to the recognition of the symbiosis of the state of me and the state of my environment. Gardening like a fool who forgets she has a body. Get the order, get the order, no beauty without order.

And then it breaks out into disorder. The uncontrollable: the rooster with the piercing crow, right now walking the fence, the absolute perfection of his roosterness, perched on the post, readying for his night perch in the tree, and preparing to shriek me awake in the night. My disorder, not his.

If I could control everything, I would have nothing to do once I succeeded. No fun there.

I think both Jung and Maslow are right. We have both the drive to power and the drive to the best of oneself.

And Elvis is truly King. (listening to Blue Moon right now)

June 9, 2006

I do not allow my sentimental heart rule me. Wow, that was easy to say. Probably the start of my first novel, but not true of me, not by a long shot.

Last night I dreamt I went to Manderly again. My one unrealized goal in life is to write an opening line like that.

Both joy and panic about the garden being only fifty hours from a semblance of control. Sheep will be sheared in two weeks. The doors will be back on their hinges after the carpet laying. Organizing the garage is a big project, but will be done.

And then what? Well, of course, continual maintenance. But will I really be the *grande dame* in the perfect place that I have created for myself in order to be the Grande Dame of someplace, anyplace (or at least a fast, wild, strong wiry cowboy).

I read a wonderful column by John Krist who contributes columns to *Writers on the Range*.

He spoke of letting go of the "connected" world, the world of other people and ordinary reality by floating on a river. The place he describes makes me cry at its beauty: a river gorge in the middle of the desert. But the oddest thing, I felt scared, a little strangled, thinking of being in that free place. So completely free. And alone, possibly. Maybe the canyon walls would collapse on me. And I would never have a chance to say good-bye.

Having it all isn't as wonderful as those who do not, might think. Well, of course, Janis again, *Freedom's just another word for nothing left to lose* – over and over the reminder that freedom entails sacrifice, more than I am willing to give. All the ties that bind, and sometimes chafe, are emotional.

I wonder if this is what makes it so hard—being bound in love both to my memories of Dave and the reality of him now.

Well, this existential mode I am in makes me really nervous. Best go out and pull some weeds rather than sit here and listen to Elvis and remember what it was like to be thirteen. And cry knowing that it won't be long before I will lose too much.

Chapter 35

JUNE 19, 2006

If it keeps on raining the levee is going to break.
When the levee breaks, it's sure goin' to break on me
—Led Zeppelin

It broke, or seeped, last night.

Patrick, Katie and boys here. P and K working overtime to help us. Patrick finishing the trench for the water pipe so we would no longer be dependent on a hose, as we had for the last four years, to bring water to the house. Cutting the bottom of the doors to fit the new carpet. The boys, sorting the recycles.

Katie doing all the cooking and hours today on the clean up.

Kathy working to the bone on her new business, really, to the bone. I can see it.

Then last night Roxy came for dinner. She had been staying a couple of months with her brother. Her Bi-polarness is more than any of us can take sometimes. Compassion is my middle name; craziness my nemesis. I was gone for a moment. Came back to find that she had left, feeling "not welcome."

I guess she was right. I once loved her enthusiasm, her competence – she knows a lot about a lot. She always listened, not just waiting to say the next word—though even from the beginning I often did not understand what she was talking about. So much manic, even though on meds—that's the part that makes me crazy too these days. Maybe she will get better and we will *see* each other again.

Then, not too much longer after that, and Kathy had left, Patrick came to me to say that Dave had a bathroom incident. What I first saw was a toilet smarming and a waste basket full of toilet water... some kitchen bowls full of water and papers. Seemed dealable. Then I looked in the sink. Oh shit. Yes, oh Shit. A huge pile of it. Apparently moved from the toilet to the sink. I asked Dave why. He said he needed to clean it before putting it back. I did not ask which item he wanted to clean.

Bless his heart, my darling David is doing all he can to be in our life—and to make sense of his. I cannot begin to imagine his world. What is he thinking when he tries to remove imaginary threads from his fingers—though I am only supposing they are threads because of his motions.

Now not only can he not put the words together to tell me what is going on, he speaks so quietly I have a hard time hearing him. Apparently this is another symptom of the disease; how hard this is for me, wanting so much to learn what he has to say but not wanting to pester him, let alone make him feel badly for something he can't help.

June 20, 2006

Depressed all morning, worried that I had alienated Kathy. About Roxy she had angrily said, "She is a human being."

I pride myself on being kind to others. Blew it, apparently, though I don't know exactly how. Katie surmised it was my attitude: irritated, snappy, the slit of my eyes, the hardness of my mouth.

Kathy and I talked this afternoon, I crying, apologetic, so (to her) clearly overwhelmed. She said, "You always seem so okay, handling it, that I forget how hard it really must be." That she was sorry for things being so hard.

Yes, and they are. I feel hugely burdened sometimes.

When my sister and I were sitting on the little bench in front of the fireplace in our Arcadia house years ago, fantasizing about living in the country, she said, "You can't be a farm woman unless you can catch a rabbit and kill it with your bare hands."

Boy, was she right about that. I, who cannot in good conscience kill a Black Widow, let alone a harmless spider, seem to have no compunction about wiping out a human being with a word, a look.

I am a killer protector of my family. Deal with it y'all.

There is that damn shearing to go. Kathy wanted to come over here at three (as though she has spare time) to help set up the barn. I have been so exhausted that I hadn't pulled it together by 2:30, so cancelled. Dave and I will do it tomorrow. Or postpone the shearing to next week. Possibly annoying the shearer and subjecting the poor animals to another seven days of being uncomfortably hot.

Little did I realize five years ago how multi-dimensional this loss is. At that time I had a glimmer of the emotional impact but not the physical. Few outside this small circle of Alzheimer's families realize how much besides memory is affected. The loss of ability to function physically because of both waning strength and loss of realistic spatial reckoning is a huge problem.

June 21, 2006

Day off. Kathy, worried about me, cancelled *Grandma Day*, had Simone do a whole day at school, because she thought I needed a real break. She was right. Lay on the couch all day, finished one book, half way through another.

Oh yes, go away world. For just this little bit.

June 23, 2006

Hey wee one, m' lil bairn what is trubling yu now?

Well, yu know, already, Da, that I have all the worl' on my shulders.

Well, m'darlin' daughter, this is not a tru thing. Yu hev only yur world on your shulders.

But, Da, e'en so, how do I cary it?

Ah, little one, yu know the answr. Pet your husban' on the head, pet yur dog, luv your friends, an be a fierce protector of yur children.

And remember what your dentist said, that what is happening in your mouth would make anyone a basket case, and you are not the "basket case type."

And all this time I thought it was my life, instead it's only a tooth.

Well, on to the next challenge!

June 25, 2006

Oh how I wish I could go back to those ivory towers, sitting in classes, discussing ideas. Little idea, or too much idea, about how it all played out, the esoteric subjects of pure thought.

I did so much, want to go to Rami Shapiro's workshop. He is a great Jewish mystical teacher with big ideas.

I was monitoring D before I left for his okayness. He was in one of his foggy states. Kept putting the mailing labels on top of each other instead of on the postcards. I kept an eye on him for a few minutes, then took a shower, getting ready. Said to myself, okay, if he does it one more time, I won't go.

Well, he did. So I didn't.

June 26, 2006

Our 30th anniversary. It was so hot that day, as it is today. We didn't care. In that wooden chapel, his face dripping, my thighs also.

We were so in love. In passion, in hope, shared idea that life should be a lot of fun, few restrictions. His rule was that you could do anything you want except piss on the floor. What a huge change from the authoritarianism of my step father and Thomas. Not that Dave made the rules in our family, I did, but he set the pace. A pace which gave me the freedom.

We sure went for it. One of the things I remember is how I flew down the aisle to the wedding march—I wanted to get there. Dr. Roberts, the minister, waved his hand at the organist to quit the wedding march, I was already next to my groom. The kids on either side; the girls on mine, Patrick the best man. It was arranged that I would hand the bouquet to Kathy, Jennifer would give the ring, Dave's ring to me. Patrick my ring to Dave. It was incredibly sweet.

The party after, now that I think of it, amazing how bare-bones basic and how joyful. Sawdust…sawdust and heat. And music from an old cassette player. We would have used paper plates if Mother hadn't intervened. We didn't care. We were in love. We had a new life coming.

June 28, 2006

Yesterday was a marathon of heavy physical work to get the four jobs done:

1. Prep the barn for shearing
2. Rainey's for food
3. Mailings, at least 200
4. Post office, pharmacy and library

Three accomplished. Cleaning the barn wiped me out. I was up at 5:30, Rainey's by 7, in the barn by eight. Dave still asleep.

Later he helped in the barn a bit but saw each wheelbarrow load as a hurdle.

And also, I was back and forth, back and forth, moving hoses, watering, watering in the awful heat.

This morning woke at four-thirty. Finally got up at five. So much to do, so much to do. Dishes, laundry, keeping Dave on track, the mailings, and the infernal pressure of the shearing. The sheep are hot. I am trapped between my responsibility, my obligations, and my powerlessness.

Trekking, trekking up and down the pastures, the yards, coercing the rams to come to where they need to be. Closing gates, convincing llamas to stay where they are. Bringing in corn for the first time in years, unloading the corn from the car, heavy, Dave did that and nearly buckled. (Earlier today Kathy took away our many bags of recyclables and did not buckle. I used to be forty-four with all that strength.)

Simone here, carving out a little more of my strength.

Later, offering the rams corn to come into the yard makes it easy because they remembered the sound of the corn in the tin bucket, charging, nearly charging. Especially Tag Along, bottle baby, now eight, no fear of me, wants what he wants. 250 pounds of wanting what he wants. Cannot let Dave help with this, he would be easily bowled over. A bit unsteady now.

How did I get here? Was it so long ago Daddy, Dave and I were eating lunch at Claridges? Most amazing mushroom soup. No, wait, Claridges was High Tea. The lunch was somewhere over looking the Thames. Oh well.

I'll think of it.

Last night I dreamed I went to Manderly again…

Chapter 36

June 30, 2006

Well, me an' my new frien' John did it! Sheared them sheep.

Got em in las' night, racing the rain. I am a wild woman. Back and forth, back and forth, seducing the ole and shy ones, a handful of corn. Come with me, come with me.

John here at seven fifteen this morning, close to the promise. Motorcycle and kit.

Today I realized I have this terrific survival trick. Although an amazing optimist and idealist (my own survival courses, of course), I have this other tool: expect the worst. The real then becomes such a jewel.

John was a jewel, all the competency and even temperament you want in a shearer. My worrying that he sounded old and had no teeth had nothing to do with what he is.

Grow up, grow up Michelle, King Kong is not outside your window.

Ah, but he was, when I was five at Grandma's and the water sloshed in the swimming pool, and then when Mommy and Daddy were gone away, he was looking in my window. I saw him, truly.

Then the baby sitter drew me to her, back to back. I fell asleep. Oh poor little rich girl. They brought you a poodle, Demi-Tasse. When Mommy and Daddy separated, they took him away. They (she, actually), were always taking animals away from me. Well,

I showed them, didn't I? I have more animals than any sane person in my circumstance would have.

Did I say sane? Whoops.

After the shearing, moving sheep, opening, closing gates, this little bubble, flutter, of euphoria was bouncing around my diaphragm. It is just a flutter, like the beginning of an orgasm, but will burst in the next couple of days. The rest of the summer is mine. The garden now has my full attention. I can revel in my paradise.

July 1, 2006

I am listening, over and over to a song, *The Ladder*, Alejandro Escovedo. It is about connection to a lost one. Extraordinary in melody and lyrics for evoking its theme. *This ladder climbs from me to you.*

Reminds me of the ladder Jacob encountered, the angels ascending and descending. One of my favorite Torah portions. Another favorite, this week's portion, the spies. What were they thinking of, to be so afraid? God wanted them to go out to see how fine the land was for the settling. They saw their own fears, projecting, as I do so well.

Don't know I think so much of God, but Torah is pretty wonderful.

My darling niece Gemini is birthing her baby Jack today. Started labor at 4 this morning, Eight centimeters now, 7:30 pm. Another member of the Montgomery-Hamilton-Hart clan. Each one so welcome, so loved. And the one slowly leaving, always loved, always in our shared memories of him.

My life is good and rich because of family. I tell people about Dave's 'disability' so they will understand him, not for sympathy for myself. It is just so right out here among farmers, they know the cycles of life, live it every day; and they all know him. No one says, "Well this must be hard for you." They say things like, "So, you left your friend home today." "Hi Dave, how yer doin?" "Hey, how are you two?"

This is what I do now. It is no big deal. Well, a bit of a deal.

July 2, 2006

Someone died a little bit today, I think it was me. I lost my fantasy love. Turned out to be only my projection. A testament to how much need fires the imagination. I will never be in love again. I will never have joyous sex again. I am old. I am old, probably dying. Well why wouldn't I be? I smoke, drink, and do the hoochey kooch.

I have lines on my face, and like Rock and Roll, especially Elvis, especially the Stones and Neil Young, Lynard Skynard, Led Zep.

I will go back again, go back in a story. It will be a story about people who did not realize their children were also real people. These parents cared about their children, but from time to time forgot to notice them.

It will be about a loving father who was weak. A step-father who was too strong. The mother is complex, needs development. The teenage heroine marries a mystery man who becomes a megalomaniac. They have three children, whom she protects with ever fiber.

She later marries a good man who becomes mentally disabled after twenty-five years of marriage.

This man, hearing the news of Gemini's new baby, says, "That's a big deal, I must have gone through that with my child, but I don't remember." He has no birth child, never went through it.

I had a dream last night that I was supposed to put some substance on one of my dogs to cure her of something or other and light a match to it. It seemed it would be the cure, but I held off, over and over, I held off. I knew she would be consumed.

I have no problem whatever understanding why people commit suicide. What I do not understand is why more do not.

Hey, missy, take an extra pill.

August 2, 2006

There is an advantage to this box I am in. Routine, routine, routine. I love the control of meeting specific goals. Right now, 6 or so AM, I get the coffee, turn on the computer. Look out on the day. Feed the animals: sheep, dogs, cats, chickens, birds. Household stuff, dishes, laundry, bed making, etc, etc. Dave can do none of it now. Not even the mowing, because of his infected foot and the bruised elbow from falling Saturday. Or the deck sweeping, which he loves.

Panic if there is somewhere I have to go. Walk it through: I have two hours until I have to shower, allow ten extra minutes to drive by Rainey's to check the tires, a feckless, needless addition to a car that can fly.

Wait for D to wake, reveling in the silence, and the lack of demand. But tense to what will be coming soon. Has he fallen again? Have his wounds healed? Do we need to go to the doctor, the pharmacy today? Does the scattered glass before my eyes have to be knocked away again for a few hours?

My friend Cathleen wrote this today: *It must be a challenge to be with what is, rather than wanting what was.* I appreciate that kindness. In truth, I have so many friends, but allow in only a few.

August 3, 2006

Well apparently getting old really "ain't for sissies." We got a card from Dave's old friend Lou Preston letting us know his wife of over fifty years, Jan, had died. They were all friends, musician friends, in LA in the fifties.

Lou sounded so old. Well, I guess he is old. And grieving. I called him as Dave would not know how to deal—any connection except with our most intimates makes him anxious. He claimed he had not spoken with Lou in 25 years. Not true. Plus Lou sends a holiday card with picture each year.

He was so happy to hear from us, not at all sure where Dave had gotten to. Now I think I should call Buddy Baggish, Lee Stacle, Steve Franken, Lee Katzen (no, Lee is dead) Lou Ciotti. His old buds.

I wonder what happened to my friends from days gone by. I could probably find them but for this convention of taking the name of the man you marry. Stupid idea. Dave can find his friends, I cannot. A little bit of social evolution nuttiness, redeemed in this next generation, I sincerely hope.

I am not old, just a little grey. I am strong, wielding the mega pruner clipper thing Roxy brought, like Paul Bunyan. The pruning saw is an extension of my arm. The chain saw is back home. I cannot wait to clean it up and go after all that needs to be cleared away.

I am woman: do not fuck with me!

And on the lighter side, barn dance at Rainey's Sat night. Our neighbors are going, as are Kathy, Roxy and Simone. I am them, I am them, I am them. What a relief to find my place.

I am never going to Cap D'Antibe again. I will never wear a bikini again. Putting on eyeliner and mascara is so tedious. Hotel George V? Not likely.

I would like to sit once more in the Oak Bar at the Plaza, however. The realization I could just jump on a plane and do that is dizzying. I know exactly which booth, and then go to the Oak Room for dinner. Order the (forbidden) veal chop with asparagus.

I could do that tomorrow. Trippy. And why not?

August 5, 2006

We just got back from the barn dance at Rainey's. Much more fun than TV. Good rockabilly sort of band with a dynamite fiddle player. Dave and I, Kathy and Rox and Simone danced our feet off. There were no other dancers between age twelve and sixty. Only the very young and the very old seemed fully alive.

Huge crowd, however. I am now divested of my egalitarian romantic fantasy. *We are definitely not them.*

Egads, I am the elitist I tried to escape.

Who are these scruffy, lanky men? Who are all these people who frown in the face of wonderful music? Why are they sitting still? Don't they see the children who are up dancing, laughing, crazy in love with life? What happened to them? What happened to me that I laugh and laugh?

Earlier today wild turkeys came. Never before. Simone moved toward them, I stopped her. They needed to fly over the fence, stay with their flock. Very tense, many left behind. Finally most made it over. One left behind, I went out to open a gate, tried to figure out how to get her back with her people. Simone yelled from the deck, "Grandma, why are you going up the road?" I could not tell her until I was back that I was trying to save the one. I opened a gate, but he flew over.

I feel these things as a real pain. Back behind my eyes where the tears start. I do not know what to do with struggling humans. I inure myself. It is always the one human. Other than the children,

I care only briefly about the hundreds of Lebanese who have died. I want *my* people to live. There is monstrousness out there that is too hard to look at and digest.

What I want is the wild turkey to fly over the fence and make it back to life.

August 6, 2006

Two rams dead today. One, my bottle baby, Tag Along. Seven or eight, about the age rams drop dead.

But I am not there. I noticed him missing yesterday. Not missing exactly, just not with the other rams who came up to greet Simone and me. I saw a vulture circling yesterday. It went off. When I see a vulture, I always scan the pastures. Saw nothing. A dark animal lying by the barn in yard four, but regularly obscured by a very alive llama.

I died a little today, but put up a fight. Alejandro Escovado singing again now. And again and again.

I died a little today, wondering if there was some attention I could have given that would have saved my bottle baby.

And for sure, in yard three, the old ram's leg had been trapped under a loose barn siding. Rams do not speak much. But if my life were less crazy, I might have heard his low voice, if he protested at all. Well, he is very dead now.

Called Kathy early for help moving them out into the pasture. Before they rotted. Before we could no longer pull them out because their legs would break off. She drove the truck, maneuvering perfectly, I put the rope on the legs, made sure the carcass cleared the gate. Drove to the south pasture. Found a few bones of the already dead. Brought the two boys together with the ghosts.

Vultures, those most beautiful and maligned of creatures, circled. Called their kin. The sky is full. But they never landed, even by sunset. I am guessing they are waiting for the coyotes to open the bodies, the real putrefaction to begin.

Tag Along was swarmed by wasps, Old One by flies. Even though they were only fifty feet apart. Interesting.

We are headed there Dave and I—really no sense in denying it. Perhaps the acceptance will intensify our fun at the barn dances; our joy in the first daffodils, asparagus sprout; our awe at the first rainbow.

Our lives are falling into a pattern—a certain predictability that is comforting.

I am no longer frightened as I was after Dave's diagnosis. We are *flowing* toward the end, not careening.

This life of ours is eternally present.

I am the same, I am compassionate and giving. I serve him his breakfast before I take my own.

He is the same, compassionate and giving. When I give him his coffee, he always asks, "Do you have one for yourself?"

Each meal, he says three or four times, "Great food, kid."

Each sandwich I make, I ponder the decision whether he would like it sliced diagonally or in rectangles, perhaps little squares.

There was a snow storm today. We both watched, entranced. I think our experience was not different. The same is true in autumn; each leaf falling is new to us both.

༺༻

I started this diary in anger. The anger is gone. Over these last years, acceptance has taken its place.

I am from a new place. I cherish each of the moments.

In looking back at this diary, my diary, I see that movement.

He cannot change. I can. And so it has been so much about me. My memories, tapped into for whatever reason that comes from the NOW, the time I am writing, this time in my life.

We will stay in this paradise of our farm. Our dogs and cats, llamas and sheep. Wild birds at the feeders.

Coyotes on the edge, vultures, waiting for each old one to leave.

Not Every Tree Lives

Plant against the hot drying wind,
Rail against it too.
Water wisely,
Water much.

But each has its sole ground
That was decided long ago.
You made the choice for planting,
You made the choice for life.

Now back, now back,
Go your own way.

The hot dry wind will drive some
To the ground.
The hot dry wind will drive some to the ground.

Acknowledgements

Hal Dresner, thank you for suggesting writing a journal and for your mentoring.

Much appreciation and thanks to my supportive and demanding reviewers on *The Next BigWriter* online workshop, and to Sol Nasisi for creating the Website. Special thanks to those who critiqued each chapter: Kent Bateman, Lori Bentley-Law, Jessica Chambers, Jeni Decker, Marc Delalangue, Damon, Nadine Gallo, Archie Hooten, Sara Einstein Scotti, Nancy Smith, Linda Watkins, Lesley Weston, and Patti Yaeger.

❦

I honor the amazing caregivers at Skylark Memory Care in Ashland, Oregon who not only cared for my husband with loving gentleness, but constantly encouraged me to publish my experience: Deborah, Wendy, Darla, Stacey, Scott, Christine, Tish, and the talented and empathic Director, Sandy Tracy.

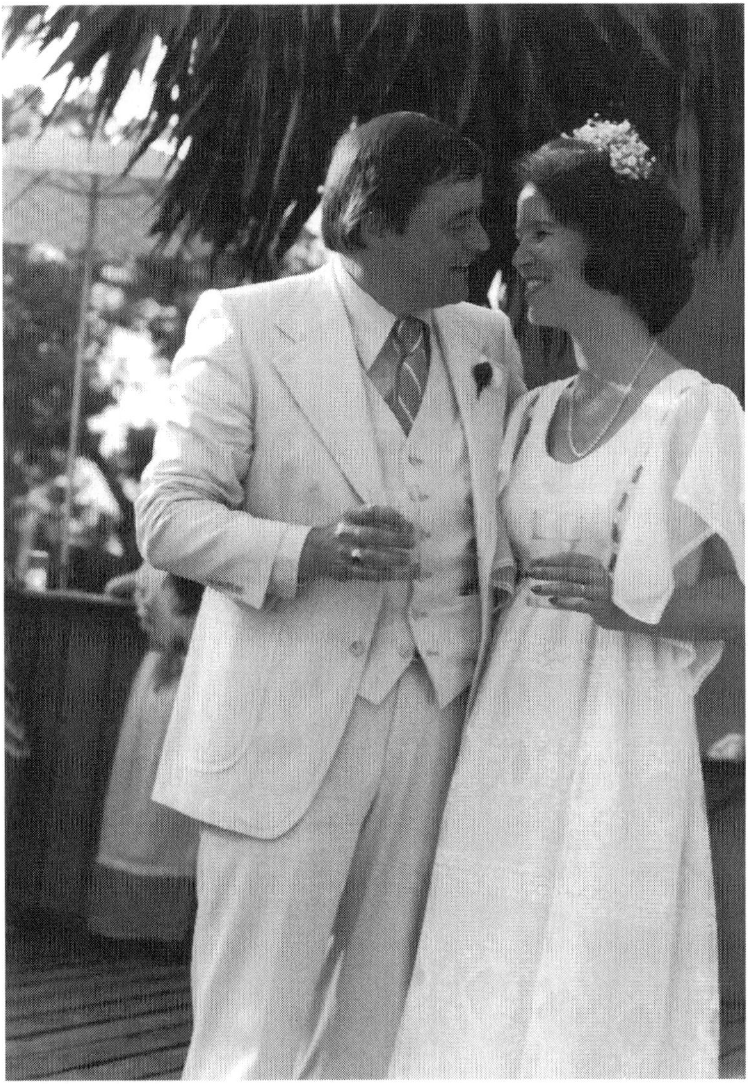

Made in the USA
Lexington, KY
31 August 2015